BEHAVIOUR MANAGEMENT TOOLKIT

A manual of good ideas and strategies for behaviour management in schools

David Koutsoukis

RIC-2809   9.5/711

Behaviour management toolkit
Revised edition

Published by R.I.C. Publications 2004
Copyright© David Koutsoukis 2004
ISBN 1 74126 065 5
RIC–2809

Additional titles available in this series:
Behaviour management posters

Internet websites
In some cases, websites or specific URLs may be recommended. While these are checked and rechecked at the time of publication, the publisher has no control over any subsequent changes which may be made to webpages. It is *strongly* recommended that the class teacher checks *all* URLs before allowing students to access them.

View all pages online
http://www.ricgroup.com.au

INTRODUCTION

Purpose

The purpose of this book is to provide a collection of practical behaviour management ideas, strategies and resources ready for use in schools. The materials have been tried and tested and, by using these 'tools', educators have the potential to save themselves hours of time 're-inventing the wheel'. It also encourages educators to be self-reflective about behaviour management issues in their own classroom or school.

Who is it for?

Whether a graduate or a school leader putting together a behaviour management plan, educators at all levels should find elements of this book useful and practical. These strategies and ideas have been developed and compiled over many years from a wide variety of schools and other sources. Research regarding current trends and best practice has been addressed in the planning of these materials.

The book has been designed as a generic resource for all types of schools and age groups. Some of the strategies would not be appropriate for certain types of schools or year levels, so it should be treated as a 'toolkit' from which you can select the tools which are appropriate, and modify them to suit your specific needs and circumstances.

Be critical

It must also be said that you may not favour some of the ideas and strategies within the book. That is fine. Be a critical thinker and use what works for you or your school. There is no 'one-best-way', so trust your own judgments and instincts. Remember that our own personalities and teaching styles are as different as the students we teach.

The 'all-day-every-day' teacher

Although I have had a variety of experiences in schools, I have spent the majority of my time as an 'all-day-every-day' teacher, and fully understand the pressures and struggles that go with it. For that reason I have kept this book as practical as possible. After a hard day at the 'chalkface', and with plenty of marking to do, the last thing you want to do is read copious amounts of behaviour management theory. You want practical solutions. Much of this book has been written in discrete sections and in point form or checklists. This has been done to enable you to retrieve quickly the information relevant to your needs.

Finally, I would like to share with you a piece of advice to take with you as you travel through the complex world of teaching kids:

NEVER LOSE YOUR SENSE OF HUMOUR AND DON'T FORGET TO HAVE SOME FUN!

Cheers and regards

David Koutsoukis

Eight dimensions of

BEHAVIOUR MANAGEMENT

This book has been divided into eight sections which I have called dimensions. Each represents a different behaviour management focus. Although there is some overlap between dimensions, they have been designed to help to facilitate easy access of materials. Find the dimension that fits your area of need and pick out the 'tools' which suit your circumstances.

(THE BIG PICTURE) **A HOLISTIC, WHOLE-SCHOOL APPROACH**

- Characteristics of schools with an effective behaviour management system
- Checklist for adopting a whole-school approach

(DIMENSION 1)
POSITIVE ENVIRONMENT

Creating a caring, safe and positive school environment
- *Developing a positive physical environment*
- *Developing a sense of involvement and belonging*
- *Developing a sense of community*
- *Acknowledging behaviour which contributes to a positive school environment*

(DIMENSION 2)
PROACTIVE PREVENTION

Proactive preventive strategies
- *Proactive prevention in the classroom*
- *Proactive prevention in the schoolyard*
- *Good teaching and learning practice*
- *Teaching of social skills*

(DIMENSION 3)
RELATIONSHIPS

Developing positive relationships
- *Teacher – Student*
- *Student – Student*
- *Teacher – Parent*
- *Teacher – Teacher*

(DIMENSION 4)
RULES AND CONSEQUENCES

Clear guidelines of acceptable behaviour and consequences
- *School codes*
- *Rewards and consequences*
- *Policy documents*

(DIMENSION 5)
ROUTINES

Procedures, roles and responsibilities for implementing a behaviour management plan
- *Roles and responsibilities*
- *Operational procedures*

(DIMENSION 6)
RESOURCES

Resources to support a behaviour management system
- *Proformas*
- *Storage and access*

(DIMENSION 7)
RESCUE AND SUPPORT

Support services infrastructure – pastoral care for students and staff
- *Support services for students*
- *Intervention and corrective strategies*
- *Support systems for staff*

(DIMENSION 8)
REVIEW

Review, reflection and planning for improvement
- *Data collection*
- *Review and reflection*
- *Planning for improvement*

CONTENTS

CONTENTS

ABOUT THE AUTHOR

David Koutsoukis is an experienced educator with over 20 years spent in schools in varying capacities. He has been a relief teacher, classroom teacher (has taught Years 1–12), head of department, behaviour management coordinator, school improvement project coordinator, middle school team leader and deputy principal.

In schools, David has developed a reputation as a dynamic and innovative person who works hard at developing strategies to provide solutions to problems. This is especially true in the area of behaviour management systems. His work is based on current research and is designed to be practical for effective use in schools.

In addition to his talents in schools, David is an accomplished entertainer and singer/songwriter. He has performed around Australia and overseas and has made many television appearances.

David is now a professional speaker and, by combining his knowledge and skills as an educator with his entertainment background, has proven himself to be a dynamic and engaging presenter. His fun and entertaining presentations cover a range of topics, including behaviour management, staff morale and motivation, team building and the importance of having fun in your life and work.

For further information about any topics or resources in this book, or for queries about presentations, contact David on:

Email   dave@funman.com.au
Web   www.funman.com.au

This book has been compiled throughout 20 years of working in schools and every endeavour has been made to acknowledge and attribute the source of materials. I would like to thank sincerely for their contribution all those people with whom I have worked with over the years on developing behaviour management systems.

Unfortunately, when collecting some of these resources the original source has been lost. I would be happy to make correct attributions in future editions.

Some of the schools which have played a part the development and trialling of these materials, or who have had an influence through the study of their behaviour management plans, include: Westfield Park Primary School, Beaconsfield Primary School, Banksia Park Primary School, Shelley Primary School, Roleystone District High School, Exmouth District High School, Mirrabooka Senior High School, Greenwood Senior High School, Leeming Senior High School, Kalamunda Senior High School and Rossmoyne Senior High School. Thanks to all these schools for their input.

At the risk of leaving someone out, I would also like to acknowledge the following people for their contribution, advice or lively discussion, which have led to the shaping of this book. In no particular order: Joe Kalajzich, Heather Gerrard, Bruce Bailey, Fred Philson, Natasha Rogers, Jodie Tomka, Kerry House, Jane Brown, Paul Huisman, Glenda Huisman, Vicki Pietropiccolo, Unnur Hermanniusson, Jenny Aramini, Aaron Harwood, Lachlan Spicer, Roger Mills, Joan Chapman, Peter Forrest, Kerry Hill, Dawn Abbott, Glenys Parkey, Brian Crossley, Laurie Smoker, Andy Neilson, Pat Watson, Mardie Gregory, Sue Matthews, Verna Splatt, Phil Judge, Peter Hamilton, Diane Johnston and Elise Moscarda.

Dedication

I would like to dedicate this book to my family; to my lovely wife, Anna, and two fun-filled boys, Sam and Matthew. They have had to endure my absence as I slaved away over a hot computer, and keep me centred and focused on what life is all about; to my mum, Gwen, who has always been there to support me in whatever I do (whether she actually likes what I am doing or not!); and to my dad, Albert, who has been the inspiration to actually write this book and who has modelled a strong work ethic which has enabled me to complete it. Love you all very much!

A HOLISTIC WHOLE-SCHOOL APPROACH

In this section:

Characteristics of schools with an effective ◄
behaviour management system

Checklist for adopting a whole-school approach ◄

Characteristics of schools with an effective behaviour management system

Developing effective behaviour management in schools is a very complex process and the effectiveness of behaviour management systems is determined by a number of factors. The following list provides a snapshot of desirable characteristics. A more detailed checklist can be found on the next page.

In order to establish effective behaviour management systems, schools should have:

A whole-school approach
- A whole-school approach to behaviour management.
- Strong collaboration and communication with all stakeholders in the development, implementation and review of the behaviour management plan.

Positive school environment
- A caring, safe and positive school environment which encourages a strong sense of belonging.

Proactive prevention
- Appropriate instructional strategies and pedagogies which are relevant, engaging, address the needs of students and cater for individual difference.
- Proactive preventive measures such as the teaching of social skills and values.
- Students are encouraged to be responsible for their behaviour and taught to make good choices.

Relationships
- Positive relationships, and a sense of mutual respect existing between members of the school community.
- Parents kept informed about their child's behaviour and progress.

Rules
- A clear set of rules and policies.
- Fair but effective consequences for those who misbehave.

Routines and roles
- Stakeholders aware of their roles and responsibilities.
- Operational procedures for the implementation of the behaviour management plan in place, and known and followed by staff.

Resources
- Sufficient resources allocated to behaviour management in the school.
- An infrastructure to manage resources.

Rescue and support
- A student support services infrastructure in place to provide intervention and corrective strategies for those who continue to misbehave, or have special needs.
- Staff support systems in place and a strong feeling of collegial support, shared power and trust existing among staff.

Review
- Review and reflection processes in place to monitor student behaviour and plan for improvement.

A HOLISTIC, WHOLE-SCHOOL APPROACH

A behaviour management system checklist

This checklist outlines desirable outcomes of an effective behaviour management system. How does your school rate? The checklist can also be used to develop or refine the aims of your behaviour management plan.

A whole-school approach	Strongly Agree	Agree	Disagree	Strongly Disagree
A comprehensive behaviour management plan is in place and embraced by the whole school.				
The plan has been collaboratively developed with input from and consultation with all stakeholders and addresses the school vision, mission or purpose statement.				
The system is flexible enough to allow for different student cohort needs, and different teaching styles, without sacrificing the consistency of a whole-school approach.				
One key person is responsible for 'driving' the behaviour management/ pastoral care system in collaboration with others (committee).				
The plan is well communicated to all stakeholders.				

Positive school environment	Strongly Agree	Agree	Disagree	Strongly Disagree
Key school initiatives and strategies (including the behaviour management plan) promote a positive ethos and are aimed at building a caring, safe and positive school environment.				
Members of the school community whose actions contribute to a caring, safe and positive school environment are recognised.				

Proactive prevention	Strongly Agree	Agree	Disagree	Strongly Disagree
Instructional strategies and learning programs are relevant and engaging. They consider 'how students learn'.				
Instructional strategies and learning programs address the needs of students and cater for individual difference.				
A caring schools/pastoral care system is in place that includes programs to teach social skills.				
Social skills are taught as part of the curriculum (health education, personal development etc).				
Students are encouraged to be responsible for their own behaviour.				
Students are taught how to make good choices.				

Positive relationships	Strongly Agree	Agree	Disagree	Strongly Disagree
Stakeholders value and work at building positive relationships with other members of the school community.				
School timetabling structures promote the development of positive relationships for both staff and students; e.g. home rooms, learning teams, students having few teachers, minimal student movement.				
The school has extracurricular activities where staff and students can interact outside the classroom environment; e.g. morning teas, sporting events, after-hours activities.				
The school works at developing strong links with parents.				
Parents are made to feel welcome when they come to the school.				
Parents are kept adequately informed of their child's behaviour and progress.				

A HOLISTIC, WHOLE-SCHOOL APPROACH

Clear rules and consequences	Strongly Agree	Agree	Disagree	Strongly Disagree
All stakeholders know their rights and responsibilities regarding the behaviour management system.				
Key procedures, rules, codes, policies and strategies are based on good practice, and are clear and known by all stakeholders including staff, students and parents.				
Consequences are effective enough for students to feel 'pain'; e.g. discomfort, loss of privileges, doing something they don't want to do, being somewhere they don't want to be.				
Consequences are applied as soon as possible/practical after the incident.				
Students who misbehave are encouraged to recognise the rights and responsibilities of individuals.				

Routines and roles	Strongly Agree	Agree	Disagree	Strongly Disagree
All stakeholders know their roles and responsibilities regarding the behaviour management system.				
Key procedures are clear and known by all staff.				
These procedures and practices are implemented consistently across the whole school.				
Procedures are in place to resolve conflict in a positive manner.				

Resources	Strongly Agree	Agree	Disagree	Strongly Disagree
Sufficient resources have been allocated to behaviour management; e.g. personnel and funds.				
An infrastructure is in place which organises behaviour management resources efficiently (e.g. resource production and storage, policy access).				

Rescue and support	Strongly Agree	Agree	Disagree	Strongly Disagree
All students have a specific staff member to monitor their progress and pastoral care needs, and who liaises with the student support services team and parents; e.g. home room teacher.				
Students have individual needs catered for (learning and pastoral care).				
A strong student services network (personnel to assist students with behavioural and/or other problems) exists within the school and is supported by outside agencies.				
Students at risk are identified and intervention and corrective strategies are implemented to assist them.				
Staff welfare is a priority and staff have a strong sense of collegiality, shared power and trust. They feel well supported by school leaders and other staff.				
Planning processes enable staff to confront and resolve issues and conflict, and to feel ownership of the behaviour management system and other school processes.				
Behaviour management/pastoral care duties are spread equitably among staff.				
Staff have adequate resources and professional development on behaviour management.				

Review and reflection processes	Strongly Agree	Agree	Disagree	Strongly Disagree
Review and reflection practices are in place in order to plan for improvement.				
Data are collected and reported upon to monitor the effectiveness of the system				
A committee exists which monitors the 'tone' of the school, including student behaviour and staff morale, and plans for improvement.				

THE BIG PICTURE

A whole-school behaviour management plan includes:	Strongly Agree	Agree	Disagree	Strongly Disagree
a rationale/policy statement/mission/aims				
user friendly definitions				
preventive measures				
rules, rights and responsibilities				
roles and responsibilities of staff				
routines and specific processes				
intervention strategies and corrective measures				
repairing and rebuilding strategies				
review schedules and processes				

The plan is driven by:	Strongly Agree	Agree	Disagree	Strongly Disagree
a key person responsible for the area of behaviour management				
a committee				

The committee ensures:	Strongly Agree	Agree	Disagree	Strongly Disagree
communication and consultation with all stakeholders regarding plan development and implementation				
the induction of new staff and relief teachers				

The plan is based on information gathered from:	Strongly Agree	Agree	Disagree	Strongly Disagree
students – surveys, interviews, discussion groups				
staff – surveys, discussion				
parents – surveys, information forums				
other data, such as school behaviour management statistics				

The plan has been collaboratively developed by:	Strongly Agree	Agree	Disagree	Strongly Disagree
staff				
students				
parents				
members of the wider community				

The plan (or extracts from it) can be found:	Strongly Agree	Agree	Disagree	Strongly Disagree
in the staff resource file and/or information handbook				
in the parent information handbook				
in student diaries				
In information pamphlets				
on posters around the school				

The plan is communicated and reinforced:	Strongly Agree	Agree	Disagree	Strongly Disagree
in the school newsletter				
in special publications				
in classrooms				
in the schoolyard				
at assemblies				
over the PA system				

The plan is evaluated by:	Strongly Agree	Agree	Disagree	Strongly Disagree
setting review dates and processes				
collecting data from staff, student and parent surveys				
collecting data from behaviour management statistics				
analysing data and making recommendations				

FUNMAN SAYS:

A mother was sending her boy off to school.
'Mum, I don't want to go – the big kids pick on me!'
'You have to go to school', answered the mother.
'But all the teachers pick on me!'
'You have to go to school!' she said again.
'Why do I have to go?'
'You're the principal, son.'

POSITIVE ENVIRONMENT

Creating a caring, safe and positive school environment

In this section:

Developing a positive physical environment ◄

Developing a sense of involvement and belonging ◄

Developing a sense of community ◄

Acknowledging behaviour which contributes to a ◄
positive school environment

POSITIVE ENVIRONMENT

Ideas to create a caring, safe and positive school environment

One of the aims of any behaviour management system should be to create a *caring, safe and positive school environment.* Listed below are some ideas aimed at helping students, staff and parents to become *known and valued members of the school community.* Tick the box of any activity which may be appropriate for your school.

School environment

- ❏ Welcome sign at the front of the school
- ❏ Welcome mat outside classrooms or school entrance
- ❏ School vision, mission or purpose statement sign at the front of the school
- ❏ 'Adopt a spot' – classes look after a part of the school
- ☑ Classrooms neat, orderly and in good repair
- ❏ Equipment, furniture and facilities in good repair
- ❏ Best kept room award

In the classroom

- ❏ Classroom aesthetically pleasing and student-centred
- ❏ Positive message posters up in room (preferably written by students)
- ❏ Acknowledge birthdays (sticker, sing, small gift)
- ❏ Teach social skills and values
- ❏ Appropriate instructional strategies and pedagogies
- ❏ Lucky dip
- ❏ Stickers, stamps
- ❏ Prizes
- ❏ Group points
- ❏ Class raffle, lucky draws
- ❏ Lolly jar
- ❏ Marble jar
- ❏ Snakes and ladders chart
- ❏ Progress charts – records of good behaviour or achievement; e.g. credit slip tally chart
- ❏ Fast food lunch

Learning

- ❏ Appropriate, flexible curriculum
- ❏ Engaging instructional strategies
- ❏ Pedagogy which caters for different learning styles and individual needs
- ❏ Learning programs which enable students to experience some success
- ❏ Student-centred learning opportunities
- ❏ Sports education model in physical education
- ☑ Individual education plans

Recess/Lunchtime activities

- ❏ House/Faction competitions
- ❏ Sporting competitions
- ❏ Computer room
- ❏ Library
- ❏ Tutorials
- ❏ Special lunches
- ❏ Music
- ❏ Clubs
- ❏ Special projects; e.g. year book, solar car challenge.

House/Faction system

- ❏ Ongoing points system
- ❏ Reward at the end of term
- ❏ Lunchtime competitions
- ❏ Faction competitions during sport

Behaviour management plan

- ❏ Credit slips and credit slip diary stickers
- ❏ Certificates of appreciation
- ❏ Credit award medallions – for accumulating credit slips
- ❏ Letters of commendation
- ❏ End of term reward event

School-based Presentations

- ❏ Merit certificates
- ❏ Subject awards
- ❏ Certificates of appreciation
- ❏ Thankyou cards
- ❏ End of year awards – presentation night

External competitions or awards

- ❏ Awards from academic or other competitions
- ❏ TV school quiz programs
- ❏ Other special awards; e.g. Duke of Edinburgh, Pierre de Coubertin Award

Public acknowledgement/celebration of student achievement

- ❏ Acknowledgement of achievement in school newsletter
- ❏ Articles in the local papers
- ❏ Displays of student work around the school; e.g. artwork framing project, design and technology display, poster competitions, front office display, library and classroom displays
- ❏ Local shows, Royal Show
- ❏ Enter work in competitions
- ❏ Students referred to principal with examples of good work
- ❏ Honour board
- ❏ Hall of Fame (photos of special achievement)

- ❏ Whole-school assemblies
- ❏ Year group assemblies
- ❏ School website

Responsibilities (sense of purpose) for students at risk

- ❏ Help look after animals in classroom or science room or similar
- ❏ Adopt a piece of garden or bushland
- ❏ Help the gardener
- ❏ Special responsibilities in classroom

Safe haven for students at risk who may be victims

- ❏ For example, library or computer room opened at break times
- ❏ Doing jobs in a classroom or other areas
- ❏ Area near staffroom in view of staff
- ❏ Lunchtime tutorial sessions

Performance

- ❏ Musical groups
- ❏ Concerts
- ❏ Interschool festivals or competitions
- ❏ School production

Giving students responsibility

Student council or prefects

- ❏ Head boy, head girl, head prefect, student president etc.
- ❏ Regular meetings
- ❏ Running of and participation in assemblies
- ❏ Organising socials
- ❏ Flag roster
- ❏ Fundraising projects
- ❏ Year group/class/faction lunches; e.g. sausage sizzle
- ❏ Roles in special events, e.g. Anzac Day
- ❏ School decision-making group/school council representation

Other

- ❏ House or faction captains
- ❏ Monitors
- ❏ School helpers (admin. assistants/hosts) – students sit at front office for the day and do jobs as they arise

Badges or identifying clothing

For roles of responsibility, achievement or belonging to a group within the school

- ❏ Student council or prefects
- ❏ Head boy, head girl, head prefect, student president etc.
- ❏ House captains
- ❏ Band, choir
- ❏ Debating team
- ❏ Senior class; e.g. class of 2005
- ❏ Sporting teams

Cadets

- ❏ Military
- ❏ State Emergency Service
- ❏ Environment cadets
- ❏ Police/Rangers

Parents

- ❏ Parent morning teas
- ❏ 'Captain's Table' – a group of parents come in and have morning tea and chat with principal
- ❏ Framing committee – group of parents who come in and frame students' work to be displayed around the school
- ❏ Parents assist in classroom
- ❏ P&C
- ❏ School fetes
- ❏ Fundraising
- ❏ Helping maintain school equipment
- ❏ Busy bees

Community members

- ❏ Mentors program
- ❏ Volunteers program
- ❏ Service groups sponsoring awards or scholarships

Staff

Fun activities for staff and acknowledgment of efforts (see also website www.funman. com.au)

- ❏ Regular fun activities
- ❏ Secret friends
- ❏ Fun awards
- ❏ Social events

- ❏ Special lunches/morning teas
- ❏ Awards/certificates
- ❏ Acknowledge birthdays
- ❏ Collegiality Coordinator (Director of Fun!)

Year group programs

- ❏ Year coordinators program
- ❏ Year group assemblies
- ❏ Socials
- ❏ Fast food lunches
- ❏ Fundraising projects
- ❏ Camps
- ❏ Transition programs; e.g. primary/ secondary
- ❏ School ball/dinner dance

Senior students program (final year students)

- ❏ Canteen roster
- ❏ Yearbook
- ❏ Seniors' leavers shirts
- ❏ Musical production
- ❏ Fashion parade
- ❏ Work experience
- ❏ Peer support/mentoring

Self Improvement/peer support programs

- ❏ Peer support program
- ❏ Students surviving schools courses – student services.
- ❏ Self-esteem courses.
- ❏ Social skills programs; e.g. Stop, Think, Do!, Bounce Back!

Student services

School-based, district level or outside agencies

- ❏ Psychologists
- ❏ Chaplain
- ❏ School-based police officer
- ❏ Nurse
- ❏ Intervention officer
- ❏ In-school education support – for students with special needs
- ❏ Outside agencies support for students with special needs

Musical

- ❏ Recorder ensemble
- ❏ School band
- ❏ Public performance – assemblies, spring festival, other events

Sporting

- ❏ House system – interhouse sporting carnivals – swimming, athletics, cross-country – various awards and presentations
- ❏ Interschool sports competition; e.g. lightning carnivals; swimming, athletics and cross-country carnivals; after school

- ❏ Lunchtime sport competitions
- ❏ Physical education – sports education – award winners and presentations at the end of each sport unit

Extracurricular staff-student Interaction

- ❏ Staff-student joint morning teas, lunches, sausage sizzle, etc.
- ❏ Staff-student sports games

Other special events

- ❏ Night events, film nights etc.
- ❏ School holiday activities program

FUNMAN SAYS:

Did you hear about the principal who caught two kids up to mischief behind the gardener's shed?

One was drinking battery acid and the other was eating fireworks. The principal grabbed them both and called the police, who took the boys away.

He later rang the police to find out what had happened to them. The police had charged one and let the other one off!

PROACTIVE PREVENTION

Proactive prevention strategies

In this section:

Proactive prevention in the classroom ◄

Proactive prevention in the schoolyard ◄

Good teaching and learning practice ◄

Teaching of social skills and values ◄

Proactive prevention in the classroom

This checklist is designed as a self-reflective tool to give you some ideas on how to encourage good behaviour from students in your classroom. Elements of this checklist overlap with those from the 'Positive Environment' and 'Relationships' dimensions.

Encourage a safe, caring and positive learning environment	Strongly Agree	Agree	Disagree	Strongly Disagree
I encourage an environment of mutual respect.		✓		
I enforce school rules which protect the rights of others fairly and consistently.		✓		
My teaching learning environment is neat, clean, orderly.	✓	✓		
I try to maintain a sense of humour.		✓		
Fun, smiles and laughter are a regular occurrence in my classroom.		✓		
I don't embarrass students or put them down (and damage my relationship with them).		✓		
I teach social skills and how people should treat each other.		✓		
Relationships and esteem-building activities are part of the curriculum (e.g. health ed)		✓		
I put up pro-relationships signs; e.g 'No Put-down Zone'.			✓	
I encourage tolerance of individual difference.		✓		
I teach and model conflict resolution skills.			✓	
I provide students with an avenue to confront and resolve conflicts appropriately.			✓	
I look at things from a student's point of view (lesson planning and discipline).		✓		
Students are taught self-protective strategies.			✓	
I use analogies and sayings like, 'What goes around comes around'.			✓	

Encourage a sense of belonging and involvement	Strongly Agree	Agree	Disagree	Strongly Disagree
I make an effort to ensure that students feel they are known and valued members of the class and the school community.				
I do esteem-building activities which encourage students to develop a sense of identity.				
I encourage effective cooperative learning.				
I do team-building activities which promote the cohesive bonding of the class.				
I give lots of positive reinforcement and catch students being good.				
I show trust in students and give them responsibilities.				
I allow students to participate in decision-making (where appropriate).				
I allow students to develop their own space; e.g. same desks, drawers, pigeonholes.				
I encourage students to develop ownership of the classroom; e.g. give them a say in its arrangement, give them certain jobs within the room – monitors.				
I recognise and acknowledge student achievement; e.g. positive reinforcement, certificates, awards, tally charts, displays, publish work, enter competitions, send students to principal with good work.				
I put up photos of students – portraits, doing activities, special achievements.	✓			
I ensure students have a record of their progress and achievement; e.g. a portfolio.		✓		
I mention student names in newsletter whenever possible and publish examples of work.			✓	
I acknowledge birthdays; e.g. put a list on pin-up board, give out birthday stickers or chocolate, sing.			✓	
I 'buddy up' new students and take measures to make them feel welcome.				
I ensure inclusivity and social justice issues are addressed.				
I use strategies which cater for the needs of individual students, groups and classes.				
I use strategies to help individuals solve their social and relationship problems.				
I facilitate classroom meetings to try to resolve issues.				

Proactive prevention in the schoolyard

This checklist is designed to give you some ideas on how to promote positive student behaviour in the schoolyard.

Rules and routines	Strongly Agree	Agree	Disagree	Strongly Disagree
Rules regarding schoolyard behaviour are in place and known by staff and students.				
Out of bounds areas are designated and known by staff and students.				
Staff coverage of duty areas provides adequate duty of care.				
Staff movements while on duty are not predictable.				
Staff are aware of duty responsibilities and know 'the next step' regarding procedures for managing schoolyard behaviour.				
Staff have resources available to carry while on duty; e.g. 'bum bag' with basic first aid, resource file.				
Students know who to see or where to go in the event of an incident.				

Preventing trouble	Strongly Agree	Agree	Disagree	Strongly Disagree
A variety of equipment is available for student use.				
There is an adequate amount of equipment available for student use.				
There is a variety of activities for students to do during breaks; e.g. library, computer room, sports.				
There is an equitable use of space, equipment and facilities between gender and age groups.				
There are safe havens for potential victims; i.e. safe places for students to go.				
Older and younger students are separated where appropriate.				
The length of breaks is not too long (preventing problems towards the end of breaks).				
The influence of outside factors is minimised; e.g. shops, car parks, pedestrians.				
Trouble spots have been identified and strategies put in place to address them.				
There are no hidden areas where groups of students congregate.				
Alternative arrangements are in place for wet weather or very hot days.				

Student involvement	Strongly Agree	Agree	Disagree	Strongly Disagree
Students have been surveyed to determine what activities, equipment, other needs or problems they have during breaks.				
Students help monitor schoolyard behaviour; e.g. prefects.				
Students are involved as peer mediators.				

Review and improvement	Strongly Agree	Agree	Disagree	Strongly Disagree
Review and reflection processes regarding schoolyard behaviour are in place.				
The effectiveness of staff supervision is monitored.				
New strategies are introduced to address identified problems.				

PROACTIVE PREVENTION

Good teaching and learning practice

The following strategies can help to promote positive behaviour by minimising off-task behaviour and promoting cooperation. How do you rate?

My learning programs ...	Strongly Agree	Agree	Disagree	Strongly Disagree
engage and interest the students				
are relevant to the students				
cater for individual learning styles and needs				
challenge students but still allow them to succeed				
use methodologies which promote cooperative learning				
directly or indirectly teach social skills				
use fun to make learning enjoyable				

Contemporary curriculum guidelines identify the following principles of teaching and learning:

Good teaching and learning practice	Strongly Agree	Agree	Disagree	Strongly Disagree
I provide students with the opportunity to learn by enabling them to see and practise the processes, products, skills and values expected of them.				
I present learning experiences that amplify students' existing knowledge, skills and values while extending and challenging their status quo.				
I present meaningful learning experiences for students and actively promote action as well as reflection.				
I present motivating learning programs with clear purposes to the students.				
I present learning programs that embrace inclusivity.				
I present learning programs that promote independent, paired and group learning				
I provide a safe supportive environment that promotes effective teaching and learning.				

Teaching of social skills and values

How many times have you heard a student respond to the question 'What did you do wrong?' with 'I didn't do anything!'? In many of these cases, the student really didn't know what it was that he or she had done wrong (not all of them, mind you). I believe that by modelling and teaching appropriate social skills and values we can contribute to a positive school environment and improve student behaviour.

What are social skills?

Dr Helen McGrath (1) says that 'Social skills are those behaviours which an individual displays towards others (or in the presence of others) which:

- help the individual get what he or she wants;
- help maintain a good relationship with the other person (or persons);
- take into account the rights of the other person (or persons);
- take into account the feelings of the other person (or persons) in order to avoid alienation'.

What skills should be taught?

There are a number of different views on what social skills should be taught and each school should address its own needs. Here are two views on what social skills concepts might be appropriate.

The Education Department of South Australia (2) lists them as:

- Understanding own feelings and self-concept.
- How to communicate effectively and appropriately.
- How to work cooperatively in groups.
- How to manage and resolve conflict.
- How to solve problems and make decisions.
- How to understand my values and those of others.
- How to take effective and appropriate social action.

Dr Helen McGrath (1) lists them as:

- **'Proactive social skills** – those skills which you use to initiate or maintain a sequence of interaction; e.g. going after what you want without being aggressive, approaching and joining others.
- **Reactive social skills** – those which you use in response to another's negative behaviour or when you experience negative experiences in your life in the presence of others; e.g. saying 'no' without giving offence, good winning and losing.
- **Group social skills** – which students need to successfully interact in a group, especially a work based classroom group; e.g. sharing, taking turns, listening.
- **Friendship skills** – which are needed for starting and maintaining a friendship, including establishing common bonds, showing loyalty and alliance.
- **Negative social behaviours to be avoided** – avoiding the use of alienating and aggressive behaviour, such as put-downs, bullying, bad manners.'

How do we teach social skills and values?

Social skills can be taught in a number of ways, including:

- modelling appropriate behaviour
- incidentally during lessons; e.g. reinforcing good social skills, identifying inappropriate social behaviour.
- through structured class guidelines; e.g. collaboratively developed classroom rules.
- structured class activities; e.g. cooperative learning, class meetings.
- an ongoing daily/weekly social skills program such as the Virtues Project (see 'examples').
- as part of the curriculum; e.g. health education, personal development.

PROACTIVE PREVENTION

DIMENSION 2

- integrated into subject areas.
- incursions or excursions; e.g. play 'Bully Busters'.
- through specialised pastoral care programs; e.g. student services team, school psychologist.
- whole-school resources; e.g. videos, lesson plans.
- through whole-school guidelines; e.g. school code of behaviour, bullying and harassment policy.

Examples of programs to develop social skills

- McGrath, H. and Noble, T. (2001) *BOUNCE BACK! A classroom program for teaching students to be resilient*. Melbourne: Pearson (Longman) Australia

- McGrath, H. and Francey, S. (1991) *Friendly kids, friendly classrooms*, Melbourne: Longman Cheshire.
- Bennett, B., Rolheiser, C., Stevahn, L. (1991) Cooperative Learning: *Where the heart meets mind*. Toronto, ON: *Educational connections* – Chapter 8, Teaching social skills'.
- *Stop Think Do* – www.stopthinkdo.com
- *The Virtues Project* – www.virtuesproject. com
- *Mindmatters* – www.curriculum.edu.au/ mindmatters

Values education program

- *Values education: Developing self-esteem and citizenship*, Prim-Ed Publishing

References:

(1) McGrath, H. (2001) Developing social skills and resiliency, *Faculty of Education, Deakin University – paper presented at seminar, Perth, Western Australia*

(2) Ed Dept SA, School discipline: The management of student behaviour. *'Promoting Responsible Behaviour', 1989*

PROACTIVE PREVENTION

We need to teach good social skills.

This good social skills poster is available in full colour and in A2 form in a set of behaviour management posters also by David Koutsoukis. Available from www.behaviourmanagement.net

Good social skills poster

The good social skills poster is designed to be displayed in classrooms or used as a stimulus tool for lessons. Its purpose is to provide a checklist of focus areas a teacher can work on to help students develop skills which will see them become valued and accepted members of the community.

Using the poster in the classroom

The good social skills poster can either be permanently displayed in the classroom or used in lessons to promote class discussion.

When the poster is displayed, explain to the group that for any society to operate effectively, there needs to be certain guidelines in place so people can live together in harmony. The purpose of the good social skills poster is to give a checklist of skills which can assist us in becoming accepted and valued members of our community.

Teachers can use the poster in a number of ways:

- Have the poster permanently displayed and refer to it incidentally and in context as situations arise in the classroom; e.g. 'You showed very good manners there, just like the third social skill'.
- Use it as the basis of a lesson or an ongoing program of social skills.
- Use it to complement an existing social skills program.
- Use it to develop a class or school focus on certain issues; e.g. 'This week we will be focusing on Pointer 3—Use good manners'. If there is a relevant document to go with the section—e.g. good manners poster—you may refer to that document as well.

Explanation of each section

As mentioned previously, this poster provides a checklist of guidelines for the teaching of social skills. Each of the ten pointers represents one aspect, and by addressing as many as possible in the course of your programming, you can provide students with a well-rounded social skills education.

1. Develop self-esteem

Include self-esteem activities in your teaching program. These are activities that give students 'ego food' and make them feel good about themselves. Self-esteem activities should also include those where students have positive interaction with others. Self-esteem is related to being liked and accepted.

2. Develop good values

In the course of the school year, give your students the opportunity to participate in activities which help them develop good values so they will want to:

- respect themselves
- respect others
- value the environment
- seek knowledge
- achieve their potential
- contribute positively to society.

Teachers can also refer to the good values poster which is part of this set.

R.I.C. Publications also has a great set of values education resources with a number of programs for different Year levels. For more information, visit www.behaviourmanagement.net

3. Use good manners

Many students do not have good manners modelled at home and sometimes don't understand when teachers get upset with them. By modelling, teaching and reinforcing good manners we can help students develop their social skills. Teachers can also refer to the good manners poster which is part of this set.

4. Develop good people skills

Positive relationships with other people don't just happen. We need to be aware of our actions and how they can affect the way people perceive us. Something as simple as a smile can go a long way towards getting

people to like us. By encouraging students to think about how they look, what they do, what they say, and how they say it, we can help them develop good people skills. Teachers can also refer to the good people skills poster which is part of this set.

5. Communicate effectively with others

Communication is a major focus in most educational programs. As well as the usual communication strategies such as reading and writing, we need to teach students how to communicate effectively in a variety of social contexts. Some of these might include meeting new people, assertiveness, public speaking, etiquette in certain social situations and so on.

6. Build and maintain friendships

As mentioned in Pointer 4, good relationships don't just happen. We need to work at building and maintaining friendships. As teachers, we need to encourage students to be proactive in this area. We can help them investigate the qualities of a good friend and then work at applying these in their own friendships. As the old saying goes, 'To have a friend, you have to be a friend'.

7. Work cooperatively in groups

We need to reinforce the fact that working in groups is a skill that has to be learned and practised. If we put students into a group and say 'go for it', the results are likely to be chaotic. We need to teach students strategies for effective group work, such as taking turns, listening, encouraging, not putting people down, being clear about the role of each person, and the expected outcome the group is to deliver. These are skills that are not only useful in the classroom, but will be very useful in later life.

8. Manage and resolve conflict

Being able to manage and resolve conflict is another important skill that needs to be learned. If we can teach students strategies they can use when they find themselves in conflict with others, they will be better equipped to handle the situation. Some of these strategies might include identifying the causes of conflict, realising the negative effects, how to resolve conflict, anger management

and team work. R.I.C. Publications has a great set of classroom resource books and posters on conflict resolution. For more information, visit www.behaviourmanagement.net

9. Make good choices in challenging situations

Many students have found themselves in a situation where they have made a decision that has caused them harm or which they have regretted. We can help students make good choices in a number of ways.

We can:

- help them develop positive values, so when it comes time to make a decision they have a strong values structure upon which to base their actions
- teach them problem-solving and decision-making frameworks to help them arrive at a positive outcome
- teach them how the brain works in these situations and explain that our first instinct in challenging situations is 'fight or flight'. We need to help them work through this stage to get into the process of rational decision making.

10. Avoid anti-social behaviour

There are a certain number of students who are nice 'kids' but seem to get 'caught up with the wrong crowd'. There are also those who are just plain anti-social. Anti-social behaviour is often attributed to peer pressure, but this is not always the case. We can assist students to avoid anti-social behaviours in a number of ways.

We can:

- help them recognise what behaviours are anti-social
- make them aware of the consequences of their actions in the short and long term
- help them develop a positive values base
- teach them decision-making strategies
- get them to reassess certain friendships
- help them develop interests they can expend their energy on instead of negative behaviour.

We need to encourage good values.

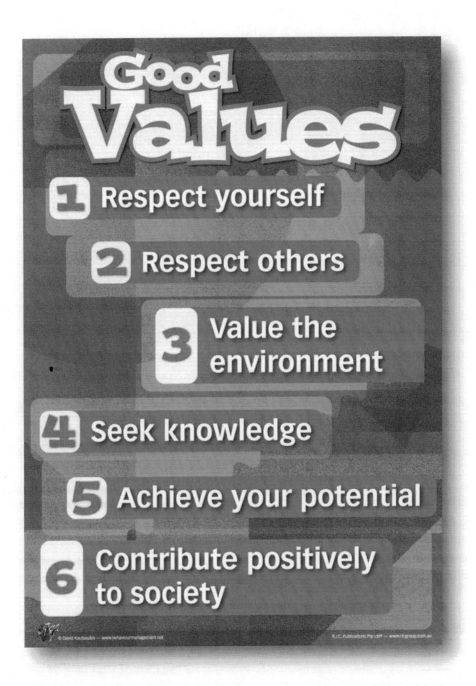

This good values poster is available in full colour and in A2 form in a set of behaviour management posters also by David Koutsoukis. Available from www.behaviourmanagement.net

Good values poster

The good values poster is designed to be displayed in classrooms, administration buildings and other prominent areas around the school and helps reinforce the purpose of any school—to develop happy, well-balanced individuals who strive to do their best and make a positive contribution to society. It can also be used in the classroom as a stimulus tool for discussion.

Using the poster in the classroom:

The good values poster can either be permanently displayed in the classroom or used in lessons to promote class discussion.

Explain to the students that an important part of being a happy and successful person is about developing intrapersonal skills. These skills involve thinking about what we do and being self-reflective about how to live a good life. Developing good values gives us a framework to guide our conscience and helps us make good choices. If we have strong values and are put in a challenging situation, we can make decisions according to those values. Developing strong values also helps address our spiritual needs and self-esteem, by giving us a sense of identity and direction.

As teachers, we need to give students the opportunity to develop good values so they will want to:

- respect themselves
- respect others
- value the environment
- seek knowledge
- achieve their potential
- contribute positively to society.

R.I.C. Publications   www.ricgroup.com.au   *Behaviour management toolkit*   33

We need to encourage the use of good manners.

This good manners poster is available in full colour and in A2 form in a set of behaviour management posters also by David Koutsoukis. Available from www.behaviourmanagement.net

Good manners poster

The good manners poster is designed to be displayed in classrooms to provide a focus for teachers and students to help them learn, and be reminded about appropriate behaviour in our society.

Using the good manners poster

Using the poster in the classroom:

The good manners poster can either be permanently displayed in the classroom or used in lessons to promote class discussion.

Explain to the group that for any society to operate effectively, there needs to be certain guidelines in place so people can live in harmony. In our society, demonstrating good manners shows you have respect for others. Displaying good manners helps us become accepted members of our community.

Teachers can use the poster in a number of ways:

- Have the poster permanently displayed and refer to it incidentally and in context as situations arise in the classroom; e.g. 'You are being very patient there, thanks for waiting your turn – just like manner number 4'.

- Use it as the basis of a lesson on manners and etiquette.

- Use it to complement an existing social skills program.

- Use it to develop a class or school focus on certain issues; e.g. 'This week we will be focusing on manner number 3—be on time'.

Explanation of each section

1. Say hello/goodbye

Greetings are an important part of our culture. A nice greeting will enhance relationships with others, while no greeting or a poor greeting can damage them. Encourage students to use a greeting whenever they meet people for the first time on any given day. Greetings may include 'hello', 'goodbye', 'good morning', 'good afternoon', 'hi', 'g'day', 'see ya' or 'ciao'! Obviously, in schools it is not practical to say something to every single person, but for those whom we know we should at least use a nod and a smile as a form of greeting.

2. Say please/thank you/excuse me

Getting permission, giving thanks and the use of apologies are important aspects of our culture. By using these protocols we are showing the person(s) we are interacting with respect and gratitude.

'Please' can be used in many ways. We should say 'Yes, please' if we are offered something; we should say 'Please may I ...?' if we want to borrow or do something; we should say 'Could you please ...?' if we want someone else to do something for us.

The use of 'thank you' is also varied. If we are given something, or given permission to do something, we should say 'thank you'. It is also appropriate to use 'thank you' when a person or a group of people has done something good or given you their attention; e.g. 'Thank you for a great effort', 'Thank you for your cooperation' or 'Thank you for your attention'.

'Excuse me' can be used in a number of ways. If we need someone's attention while he or she is busy, we should say 'excuse me' before making a point or asking a question. If a situation arises where we can't avoid walking in front of someone, or in between two people talking, we should also say 'excuse me'. It can also be used if we happen to be late, or if for some reason we burp or make some other bodily noise!

3. Be on time

Some students (and teachers) can be quite lax with their punctuality. The importance of punctuality should be outlined to students. Get them to give you some reasons why punctuality is important. The poster can be used to deal with late students in a non-emotional way:

For example, John is late and walks into the classroom.

In a polite manner the teacher says:

Teacher: *'John, could you please read out good manners number 3.'*
John: *'Be on time.'*
Teacher: *'Are you on time?'*
John: *'No'*
Teacher: *'What will you do next time?'*
John: *'Be on time.'*

4. Wait for your turn

This reinforces two points—patience and respecting others. You might give examples of where waiting for your turn is appropriate, such as lining up at the canteen, talking turns in activities or the sharing of equipment. You can also refer to the poster when students are doing the right thing and waiting their turn.

5. Sit properly

Explain to students the way we perceive people and their attitudes toward others is determined by how we look, what we do, what we say and how we say it. In the context of this pointer, the way a student sits can give a positive or negative message. If students slouch or put their feet up on a desk or chair, this is sending out the message that they don't respect the teacher. If they sit up and pay attention, they are sending out a positive message. As the old saying goes, 'what goes around comes around'. If the student is perceived to be acting in a positive manner, the teacher is more likely to be positive with him/her.

6. Ask before using

Many students these days will touch or take things without asking. This pointer helps emphasise to students the importance of asking before touching or using equipment or facilities. We can also remind them to use 'please' and 'thank you' in this instance.

7. Ask before moving

Another common issue in classrooms is students who can't stay in their seat. The good manners poster can be used to deal with students who are out of their seat in a non-emotional way:

For example, Anna is out of her seat.

Teacher: *'Excuse me, Anna, could you please read me good manners number 7?'*
Anna: *'Ask before moving.'*
Teacher: *'Did you ask?'*
Anna: *'No'*
Teacher: *'What are you going to do?'*
Anna: *'Ask' (or 'Go back to my seat.')*

8. Don't interrupt or yell out

Once again, a common problem in classrooms. Explain to students it is not appropriate to interrupt or yell out. What is appropriate is to put their hand up if they have something to say. You can use the poster as a reminder if students interrupt or yell out. 'I would just like to remind you about good manners number 8.'

9. Don't swear

This would seem straightforward, but there are some students who seem to think that swearing is acceptable. This pointer reminds them that it is not. You could even tell them that instead of swearing they should just say the number 9!

10. Don't embarrass others

It seems that some students don't understand the negative impact they have on others when they embarrass them. This may be through name-calling, teasing, put-downs or a number of other ways. We need to let students know that embarrassing others really damages their self-esteem and that's not what we want in a positive learning environment.

We need to help students develop good people skills.

This good people skills poster is available in full colour and in A2 form
in a set of behaviour management posters also by David Koutsoukis.
Available from www.behaviourmanagement.net

Good people skills poster

The good people skills poster is designed to be displayed in classrooms to provide a focus for teachers and students to help them learn, and be reminded of, strategies we can use to develop good relationships and become valued and accepted members of the community.

Using the good people skills poster

Using the poster in the classroom:

The good people skills poster can either be permanently displayed in the classroom or used in lessons to promote class discussion.

1. Smile

We should never underestimate the power of a smile. As teachers, we can explain to students that a smiling person is seen as 'likeable' and is more likely to be accepted as part of a group. Smiling also releases endorphin—a chemical that makes us feel good. If you never smile, people are going to think you are grumpy and unsociable and won't want to talk to you. Why not have a 'smile day', where everyone wears a smiley face sticker and is encouraged to smile as much as possible. I have heard of one school which had the policy that everyone (staff and students) should smile at any visitors who were in the school—what a welcome!

2. Use good manners

Explain to the group that for any society to operate effectively, there needs to be certain guidelines in place so people can live in harmony. In our society, demonstrating good manners shows you have respect for others. Displaying good manners helps us become accepted members of our community. Teachers can also refer to the good manners poster which is part of this set.

3. Acknowledge others

One thing that teachers may find annoying is students who ignore them. This may happen when they're walking through the school and say 'hello' and the student doesn't answer, or may be when they've given an instruction or asked a question and there is no response. We need to let students know how upsetting

this can be for people, and make them realise that if they ignore someone they are significantly damaging their relationship with that person.

4. Use greetings

Greetings are an important part of our culture. A nice greeting will enhance relationships with others, while no greeting or a poor greeting can damage them. Encourage students to use a greeting whenever they meet people for the first time on any given day. Greetings may include 'hello', 'goodbye', 'good morning', 'good afternoon', 'hi', 'g'day', 'see ya' or 'ciao!' Obviously, in schools it is not practical to say something to every single person, but for those whom we know, we should at least use a nod and a smile as a form of greeting.

5. Use people's names

We should explain to students that using people's names not only makes them feel good, but is also a sign you respect them. Using names is useful both in the school and wider community. Using people's names is one way you can strengthen your relationship with them.

6. Look at people when talking

Looking at people while they are talking is just one listening skill on which many students need to focus. By looking at people as they are talking, we are showing them we are interested in them and what they have to say. We should give the speaker our full attention and maintain eye contact. Having said that, it should also be acknowledged that in some cultures, looking someone in the eye is a sign of disrespect.

PROACTIVE PREVENTION

7. Listen

As the old saying goes, 'We were born with two ears and one mouth. We should use them in that order'. As teachers, we need to encourage students to develop their listening skills. Some of the strategies we can share with our students include:

When someone is speaking to us:

- Sit properly
- Give the speaker your full attention
- Look interested (facial expressions)
- Maintain eye contact with the speaker
- Don't get distracted by things going on around you
- Nod, so the speaker knows you are taking in what he or she is saying
- Don't interrupt the speaker while he or she is talking
- Ask questions about what the speaker is saying (if appropriate and after the completion of the talk).

8. Accept differences

We need to encourage our students to accept and value the amazing diversity of human beings on this planet. Just some of the range of the differences we have include:

- race
- religion
- gender
- age
- personality
- multiple intelligences (verbal–linguistic, logical–mathematical, visual–spatial, musical–rhythmic, interpersonal, intrapersonal, bodily–kinaesthetic and naturalist)
- learning styles (global learners – see the big picture, analytical – like to read the instructions)
- learning preferences (visual, audio, kinaesthetic, print-oriented, interactive)
- brain preferences (left brain, right brain)
- home life.

We need to encourage individuals to not only tolerate difference but to value it as well. We can learn so much from others with different backgrounds and personalities from ours. Other people are not weird or strange—they are just different. Isn't it great that we're all so unique!

9. Respect opinions of others

We need students to realise that just because someone has a different opinion from ours it doesn't automatically mean they are wrong. We are all a product of our own upbringings, education, knowledge and values which, of course, will differ from those of others. We need to help students recognise that it is OK to disagree with other people but still respect their right to have an opinion. It's all right to 'agree to disagree'.

10. Give compliments

To begin this section, it is appropriate to mention the opposite of giving compliments—put-downs. Some things damage relationships more than others. Put-downs and aggressive comments are certainly among the worst. On the other hand, by giving compliments we can really make people feel good. One of the biggest needs of humans is to feel important and appreciated. By giving people compliments, we can help fulfil these needs and win the respect of the person in the process.

RELATIONSHIPS

Developing relationships

In this section:

Developing relationships

Relationships can be a forgotten factor when considering behaviour management systems, but are arguably the most crucial factor. You can have the best behaviour management system in the world, but unless positive relationships exist among members of the school community, behaviour will be well below par.

These relationships include:

- Teacher–student
- Student–student
- Teacher–teacher (staff–staff)
- Teacher–parent (staff–parent)

> We need to remember that rules do not change behaviour, but positive action and interaction do. By valuing and developing positive relationships, and by implementing behaviour management procedures effectively, we can improve that interaction.

We need to work at building relationships. When we have to discipline students it should be done in a manner that will not damage our relationship with them. When rules have to be enforced, they should be done so in the 'spirit of the law' and not to the 'letter of the law'. Likewise, when sanctions or consequences are required they should be applied in an impartial and non-emotional way if possible. Students should be made to understand that they have chosen to receive that consequence as a result of their actions.

> Remember that 'Every interaction you have with others strengthens or weakens your relationship with them.' Barrie Bennett

It is unrealistic to expect all people to have perfect relationships all of the time. We are all too different for that. However, by making an effort to develop relationships most of the time we can make a significant contribution towards a caring and positive school environment, and hopefully good student behaviour.

Relationships can be improved by self-reflection on the part of teachers, school leaders, other staff and by the school as an organisation. The checklists on the following pages provide tools for this self-reflection, and appropriate strategies can be introduced according to your needs. These strategies should complement the effectiveness of your school behaviour management plan.

It should be noted that there will be some overlap with these checklists. Each of these groupings merges and interlocks with each other to make up the complex picture of relationships within a school community.

Teacher–student relationships checklist

This checklist is designed to be a self-reflective tool and to help identify areas for possible improvement. It should be remembered that we all have different personalities and teaching/ leadership styles. Some of these pointers may not suit your style. Be a critical thinker, identify relevant points and set your own goals. Some people write appropriate pointers in their journal or planner and use them as affirmations. Do what works for you!

Values	Strongly Agree	Agree	Disagree	Strongly Disagree
I value and work at building relationships among teachers and students.				
I take time to reflect on relationships in order to plan for improvement.				

How do you rate in the eyes of the students?

People skills	Strongly Agree	Agree	Disagree	Strongly Disagree
I am courteous and polite to students.				
I always acknowledge students and use their name often.				
I listen to students' points of view.				
I am caring rather than authoritarian.				
I am assertive but understanding.				
I teach social skills either directly or incidentally.				
I smile often.				

Are you a good role model?	Strongly Agree	Agree	Disagree	Strongly Disagree
I show courtesy and politeness to others.				
I am neatly dressed and well presented.				
I use appropriate language.				
I am punctual.				

Students have indicated that the following attributes are found in good teachers.

Attributes – how do you rate?	Strongly Agree	Agree	Disagree	Strongly Disagree
I have a nice personality.				
I am kind.				
I am considerate.				
I am enthusiastic.				
I am humorous.				
I have fun.				
I am fair-minded.				
I am respectful.				
I treat students as people.				
I am organised.				
I know what I am talking about (knowledgeable).				
I can teach properly (instructionally skilled)				
I can put the subject across in a way that is interesting.				
I can put the subject across in a way that can be understood.				

RELATIONSHIPS

How can I enhance relationships?

Set clear guidelines of expected behaviour	Strongly Agree	Agree	Disagree	Strongly Disagree
I ensure school codes (rules) and clearly written classroom rules are in a prominent position in the classroom.				
I enforce rules and implement behaviour management strategies consistently.				
I ensure my students know these rules and use strategies to remind them.				

Maintain high personal standards	Strongly Agree	Agree	Disagree	Strongly Disagree
I am polite and expect politeness.				
I am a good role model (I 'walk the talk').				

Try to win students over	Strongly Agree	Agree	Disagree	Strongly Disagree
I treat students as part of the team and not the 'enemy'.				
I show positive regard for students at all times.				
I always acknowledge students and give them the time of day.				
I show personal attention to every individual as often as possible.				
I make an effort to get to know parents.				

Get to know students as individuals	Strongly Agree	Agree	Disagree	Strongly Disagree
I make an effort to get to know students – hobbies, interests etc.				
I have informal chats with students.				
I participate in staff-student activities.				
I get involved in extracurricular activities.				

Show students you're human and interesting; do you?	Strongly Agree	Agree	Disagree	Strongly Disagree
tell jokes				
use humour in your lessons				
tell stories about your family				
tell them your children's or pets' names				
show them photos of your family, hobbies, or other interesting things about you				
show them any special talents you have; e.g. singing, playing an instrument				
let them know about any of your special achievements				

RELATIONSHIPS

BEHAVIOUR MANAGEMENT · **DIMENSION 3**

Teacher–student and student–student relationships checklist

Encourage a sense of belonging and involvement	Strongly Agree	Agree	Disagree	Strongly Disagree
I make an effort to ensure that students feel they are known and valued members of the class and the school community.				
I do esteem-building activities which encourage students to develop a sense of identity.				
I encourage effective cooperative learning.				
I do team-building activities which promote the cohesive bonding of the class.				
I give lots of positive reinforcement and catch students being good.				
I show trust in students and give them responsibilities.				
I allow students to participate in decision-making (where appropriate).				
I allow students to develop their own space; e.g. same desks, drawers, pigeon holes.				
I encourage students to develop ownership of the classroom; e.g. give them a say in its arrangement, give them certain jobs within the room – monitors.				
I recognise and acknowledge student achievement; e.g. positive reinforcement, certificates, awards, tally charts, displays, publish work, enter competitions, send students to principal with good work.				
I put up photos of students – portraits, doing activities, special achievements.				
I ensure students have a record of their progress and achievement; e.g. a portfolio.				
I mention student names in newsletter whenever possible and publish examples of work.				
I acknowledge birthdays; e.g. put a list on pin-up board, give out birthday stickers or chocolate, sing.				
I 'buddy up' new students and take measure to make them feel welcome.				
I ensure inclusivity and social justice issues are addressed.				
I use strategies which cater for the needs of individual students, groups and classes.				
I use strategies to help individuals solve their social and relationship problems.				
I facilitate classroom meetings to try to resolve issues.				

Encourage a safe, caring and positive learning environment	Strongly Agree	Agree	Disagree	Strongly Disagree
I encourage an environment of mutual respect.				
I enforce school rules which protect the rights of others fairly and consistently.				
My teaching learning environment is neat, clean, orderly.				
I try to maintain a sense of humour.				
Fun, smiles and laughter are a regular occurrence in my classroom.				
I don't embarrass students or put them down (and damage my relationship with them).				
I teach social skills and how people should treat each other.				
Relationships and esteem-building activities are part of the curriculum, (e.g. health ed)				
I put up pro-relationships signs; e.g. 'No Put-down Zone'.				
I encourage tolerance of individual difference.				
I teach and model conflict resolution skills.				
I provide students with an avenue to confront and resolve conflicts appropriately.				
I look at things from a student's point of view (lesson planning and discipline).				
I don't moralise and act like God.				
I use analogies and sayings like, 'What goes around comes around', 'Karma', 'The world is a mirror – smile into it and it will smile back'.				

RELATIONSHIPS

Good teaching and learning practice	Strongly Agree	Agree	Disagree	Strongly Disagree
I provide students with the opportunity to learn by enabling them to see and practise the processes, products, skills and values expected of them.				
I present learning experiences that amplify students' existing knowledge, skills and values while extending and challenging their status quo.				
I present meaningful learning experiences for students and actively promote action as well as reflection.				
I present motivating learning programs with clear purposes to the students.				
I present learning programs that embrace inclusivity.				
I present learning programs that promote independent, paired and group learning				
I provide a safe supportive environment that promotes effective teaching and learning.				

Ref: *Curriculum Council WA (1998)* Curriculum Framework, *Perth, WA*

How can I implement behaviour management strategies effectively and still maintain good relationships?

In the eyes of students am I being fair?	Strongly Agree	Agree	Disagree	Strongly Disagree
I provide students with clear guidelines as to their expected behaviour and implement consequences consistently.				
I focus on the behaviour, not the person.				
I try to deal with the problem first rather than 'pass the buck' (and give students the message that I can't control them).				
I tell the student exactly what behaviour is inappropriate as opposed to 'stop messing around'.				
I use 'I' statements; e.g. ' I want you to stay in your seat'.				
I give a specific warning before issuing a consequence when possible.				
I make students feel that getting a consequence was their own choice as a result of their actions (e.g. 'If you throw things in class again you will choose to get yourself a demerit').				
Where possible, I link consequences to the behaviour; e.g. graffiti a desk, they have to clean it				
I enforce rules in the 'spirit of the law' and not to the 'letter of the law'.				
I think about the students' perspective – 'I put myself in the other person's shoes'.				
I think about what is in it for the student to misbehave (I ask myself why are they doing it?).				
I don't engage in emotional arguments (which will give students power) and remain calm while reprimanding students.				
I avoid aggressive verbal language.				
I don't try to win at all costs (and damage a relationship in the process).				
I don't punish the whole class for something one or a few have done (and get the rest of the class offside).				
I refer students to the 'next step' if I am unable to make any progress; e.g. Year coordinator, student services.				
I follow accepted protocol regarding student conflict (bullying/harassment).				
I use strategies to help students solve their behaviour problems; i.e. reflect on their misbehaviour and implement strategies to help them change for the better.				
I ensure there is closure after a conflict so that the matter is laid to rest.				
I take time to reflect on teacher-student relationships in order to plan for improvement				

Teacher–parent (staff–parent) relationships checklist

This checklist is designed to be a self-reflective tool and to help identify areas for possible improvement. The first section looks at things you can do personally and the second looks at what the school can do to enhance relationships.

How can I enhance teacher–parent relationships?

Have regular contact with parents	Strongly Agree	Agree	Disagree	Strongly Disagree
I make regular contact with parents regarding student's behaviour and progress; e.g. note in student diary, phone call, informal chat, parent interview, parents' nights, reports, learning journeys or portfolio viewing.				
I try to mention students' names in school newsletter whenever possible and publish examples of students' work.				
I use portfolios of students' work samples to show parents student achievement.				
I invite parents to visit my classroom and learning areas.				
I organise informal parent events; e.g. morning teas.				
I invite parents to assist me in the classroom and with other school activities.				

How can the school as an organisation enhance teacher–parent relationships?

By encouraging:	Strongly Agree	Agree	Disagree	Strongly Disagree
parents to be aware of and strive to meet their obligations as members of the school community				
parents to consider the responsibility for their child's education as a partnership with the school, and support teachers and the school as much as possible				
parents to make positive comments to their children about the school and education in general, and to refrain from making negative ones (even if they think it)				
parents to be aware of their influence as role models for their children, and strive to provide a positive example to them				

By ensuring:

Good communication	Strongly Agree	Agree	Disagree	Strongly Disagree
Parents are kept well informed regarding what is happening at the school.				
Parents are happy with and understand school reporting formats and procedures.				
Parents get regular contact from teachers regarding the social and academic progress of their child.				

Positive relationships with parents	Strongly Agree	Agree	Disagree	Strongly Disagree
Parents feel welcome when visiting the school.				
Parents feel school staff are approachable.				
Parents have the opportunity to comment on the effectiveness of the school.				
Parents feel they have their views heard by the school.				
Parents have a positive perception of the school.				
Parents feel they are known and valued members of the school community.				

Teacher–teacher (staff–staff) relationships checklist

This checklist is designed to be a self-reflective tool and to help identify areas for possible improvement. The first section looks at your personal attributes and the second looks at what the school can do to enhance relationships.

How can I enhance teacher–teacher relationships?

Values	Strongly Agree	Agree	Disagree	Strongly Disagree
I am a team player. I fulfil expectations of me as a staff member and follow accepted school protocol.				
I value and work at building positive relationships with other staff and I am willing to assist them where possible.				
I am a positive role model to other staff.				
I am self-reflective and strive for improvement.				

People skills	Strongly Agree	Agree	Disagree	Strongly Disagree
I am courteous and polite to other staff.				
I always acknowledge others with a greeting.				
I listen to other people's point of view.				
I recognise, and I am tolerant of, individual difference in the leadership and teaching styles of others				
I smile often.				

How can the school as an organisation enhance teacher–teacher relationships?

Roles and responsibilities	Strongly Agree	Agree	Disagree	Strongly Disagree
Staff have a workload that is fair and equitable.				
Staff have clearly defined roles (i.e. job descriptions).				
Staff do what is expected of their job description.				
If staff aren't doing their job properly, they are assisted to do so or disciplined.				
Staff are recognised and remunerated (time, money or other) for extra duties or responsibilities.				

Pastoral care for staff (staff welfare)	Strongly Agree	Agree	Disagree	Strongly Disagree
Staff welfare is a priority.				
Staff efforts are recognised and acknowledged.				
Staff are supportive of each other.				
Staff in the classroom have strong back-up from administration.				
Staff have mechanisms in place to help build and maintain their morale.				
Staff are able to participate regularly in fun collegial activities.				
Staff who are experiencing difficulties or stress have support mechanisms available to them.				
Staff are involved in decision-making processes within the school.				
Staff feel they have their views listened to.				
Staff are aware of and follow appropriate grievance procedures.				
Staff experience equal employment opportunity and diversity practices being observed.				
Staff feel they are known and valued members of the school community.				

Resources	Strongly Agree	Agree	Disagree	Strongly Disagree
Staff as a resource are used efficiently and with minimal duplication of responsibilities.				
Staff have sufficient resources to teach effectively.				
Staff have appropriate and sufficient learning technologies available for their use.				
Staff get adequate collaborative planning time.				

Personal and professional development	Strongly Agree	Agree	Disagree	Strongly Disagree
Staff have sufficient professional development opportunities.				
Whole-school professional development days include sessions involving collegial and team-building activities.				
Staff have effective performance management practices in place.				
Staff are aware of and have professional advancement opportunities available to them.				

RULES AND CONSEQUENCES

Guidelines of acceptable behaviour and consequences

In this section:

School codes ◀

Rewards and consequences ◀

Policy documents ◀

RULES AND CONSEQUENCES

All members of the school community need to be quite clear about expected standards of behaviour.

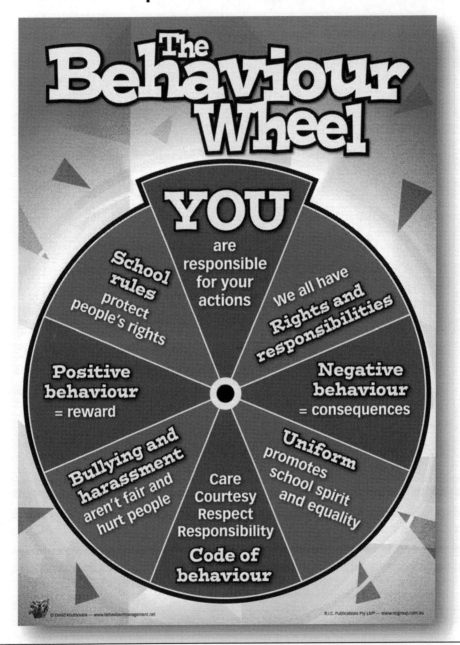

This behaviour wheel poster is available in full colour and in A2 form in a set of behaviour management posters also by David Koutsoukis. Available from www.behaviourmanagement.net

The 'Behaviour Wheel' gives an overview of main school codes. The overarching school code is the code of behaviour, and the other codes basically clarify it. Some examples of school codes can be found in this section.

School codes can be printed in colour, laminated and put up around the school as appropriate. All staff should have copies of the codes in their resource file for ready access.

The behaviour wheel poster

The behaviour management wheel poster is designed to be displayed in classrooms, administration buildings and other prominent areas around the school and provides a framework to clarify the ethos behind behaviour-management processes in schools. It emphasises that, ultimately, students are responsible for their own behaviour. As well as being displayed around the school, the poster can also be used at assemblies or for parent information sessions. The wheel is divided into sections which provide a rationale for various aspects of behaviour management systems. In some schools these sections may be backed up by codes or policies; e.g. school uniform code or bullying and harassment policy.

Using the behaviour wheel poster

Using the poster in classrooms, at assemblies or for parent meetings:

Explain to the group that for any organisation to operate smoothly, there needs to be certain guidelines in place so everyone is clear about expected standards of behaviour. The purpose of the behaviour wheel is to clarify and explain the reasons behind these guidelines. You can go through and explain each of the eight sections, or just focus on one or two. If there is a relevant document to go with the section—e.g. a bullying and harassment policy—you may go through that document as well.

Explaining each section

Section: YOU are responsible for your actions

Explain to students and/or parents that people have choices in the way they behave and the ultimate responsibility for their behaviour lies with themselves. A core aim of any successful behaviour management system is to encourage students to be responsible for their actions and to make good choices.

Section: Code of behaviour

The code of behaviour provides a 'big picture' of desirable behaviour in schools. It gives us four key values towards which all members of the school community should strive. The alliteration of 'Care, Courtesy, Respect and Responsibility' provides a 'catch cry' which becomes embedded as part of the school's ethos. The four keywords can be reinforced across the school and promote a whole-school approach to behaviour management.

Teachers can use these keywords to reinforce a student's actions when he or she is displaying positive behaviour; e.g. 'I appreciate the care you were showing for others today'. They can also be used to remind a student when he or she is behaving inappropriately; e.g. 'You weren't showing much courtesy when you pushed your way into the classroom'.

Teachers can also use the keywords to set a focus for the day or week; e.g. This week's focus is 'Responsibility'. The teacher may give out awards for students who are displaying responsible behaviour and encourage those students who have problems with responsibility to make better choices.

Section: School rules protect people's rights

Just like the 'laws of the land', schools need rules to protect people's rights. To complement the code of behaviour, we have school rules which give us more specific details about acceptable behaviour. We need this 'fine print' to clarify certain points for teachers and students. You might like to refer to your own school rules at this point.

Section: Rights and responsibilities

We know that people in schools have rights, and the school rules are there to protect those rights. Just as we have rights, we also have responsibilities. People are often very quick to remember their rights but forget their responsibilities. If your school has a set of rights and responsibilities you could go through them with the audience. Alternatively, you can use the set on the following page.

Members of the school community have the right to:

- be treated with courtesy and respect
- work in and enjoy a safe, secure and clean working environment
- teach and learn without disruption
- achieve their educational potential
- have their property respected
- be proud of their achievements.

Members of the school community have the responsibility to:

- show respect and courtesy to others
- keep the environment safe, secure and clean
- ensure there is no disruption to another person's teaching/learning environment
- develop their potential and to assist others in doing the same
- respect student, staff and school property
- ensure their actions do not discredit the school.

Section: Positive behaviour = reward

Students need to realise that their actions have consequences which can either be positive or negative. Many teachers use rewards to encourage good behaviour. Despite there being some debate on the use of rewards, most teachers would agree that rewards can be effective. It must be noted that it is a dangerous practice to 'bribe' students or manipulate their behaviour through the use of rewards. They may choose to behave appropriately only if they get something, and some would argue this diminishes their intrinsic motivation to cooperate and learn. As a general rule, it is better to use rewards as a sign of appreciation. My view is that you should do what works for you and sits well with your values.

In explaining this section to students, it should be made quite clear that 'reward' doesn't just mean 'getting something'. It also refers to the positives that come from behaving well, such as the great self-esteem boost we get from cooperating, achieving and feeling like we belong.

Section: Negative behaviour = consequences

In the last section we mentioned that students need to realise that their actions have consequences—either good or bad. Negative behaviour will mean negative consequences. Students need to know if they misbehave they will have to experience some discomfort, miss out on some of the 'good stuff' or do things they don't like to do. The great news is they get to choose whether they receive negative consequences or not! They can choose to behave well and enjoy their time at school, or choose to misbehave and face the consequences.

Section: Bullying and harassment

School rules cover most areas of acceptable behaviour. However, we need to have a separate policy for bullying and harassment because sometimes it can be very subtle, and is often hard to categorise under general school rules; e.g. nasty looks or gestures, following people or isolating them from the group. The purpose of a bullying and harassment policy is not necessarily to inflict punishment on the person bullying, but to get all parties involved to 'work it out' to resolve the conflict and move on.

Section: Uniform

Many teachers would agree that trying to get students to wear school uniform can be a difficult task. Students will often ask 'Why do we have to wear a uniform?' This section helps provide the answer. As well as the information on the poster, you might like to add that wearing a school uniform:

- gives students a sense of belonging
- instils pride in the school
- promotes a sense of equality among students
- prepares students for the future, as many work situations have dress and safety codes.

Code of behaviour/conduct – version 1

The code of behaviour provides a 'big picture' view of expected behaviour in schools.

This code of behaviour poster is available in full colour and in A2 form in a set of behaviour management posters also by David Koutsoukis. Available from www.behaviourmanagement.net

Code of behaviour poster

The code of behaviour poster is designed to be displayed in classrooms, administration buildings and other prominent areas around the school and provides a framework to clarify expected behaviour in schools. It can also be used at assemblies, for parent information sessions or in classroom lessons.

Using the code of behaviour poster

Using the poster in classrooms, at assemblies or for parent meetings:

When the poster is displayed, an outline of its purpose should be given to the audience. Explain to the group that for any organisation to operate smoothly, there needs to be certain guidelines in place so everyone is clear about expected standards of behaviour. The purpose of the code of behaviour is to provide a 'big picture' of desirable behaviour in schools. It gives us four key values towards which all members of the school community should strive. The alliteration of 'Care, Courtesy, Respect and Responsibility' provides a 'catch cry' which becomes embedded as part of the school's ethos. The four keywords can be reinforced across the school and promote a whole-school approach to behaviour management.

Teachers can use these keywords to reinforce a student's actions when he or she is displaying positive behaviour; e.g. 'I appreciate the care you were showing for others today'. They can also be used to remind a student when he or she is behaving inappropriately; e.g. 'You weren't showing much courtesy when you pushed your way into the classroom'.

Teachers can also use the keywords to set a focus for the day or week; e.g. This week's focus is 'Responsibility'. The teacher may give out awards for students who are displaying responsible behaviour and encourage those students who have problems with responsibility to make better choices.

Keyword sign: *Can be printed on bright paper, laminated and put up in classrooms and around the school to reinforce a positive ethos.*

Keyword sign: *Can be printed on bright paper, laminated and put up in classrooms and around the school to reinforce a positive ethos.*

Keyword sign: Can be printed on bright paper, laminated and put up in classrooms and around the school to reinforce a positive ethos.

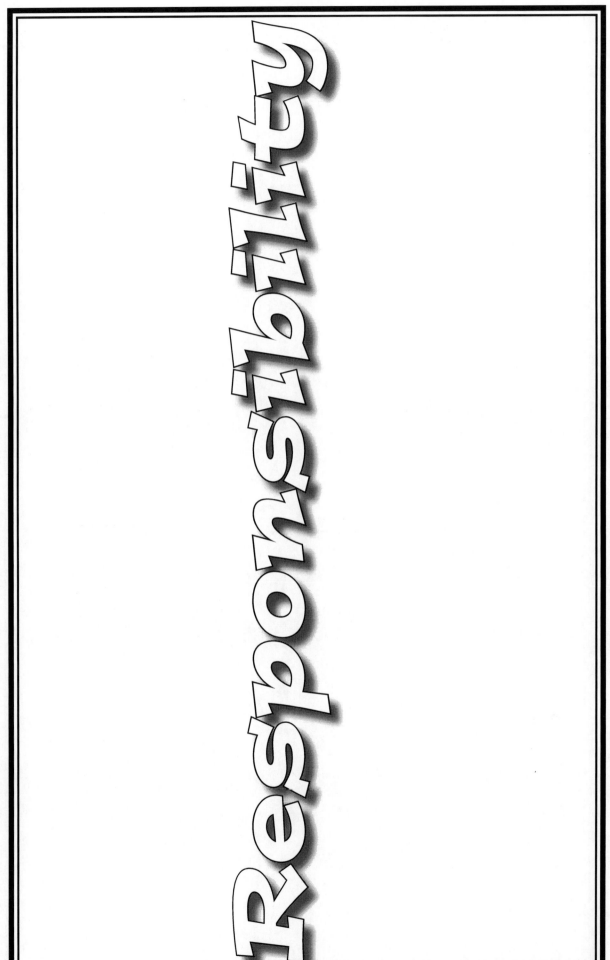

Keyword sign: *Can be printed on bright paper, laminated and put up in classrooms and around the school to reinforce a positive ethos.*

Code of behaviour/conduct – version 2

Students must:

- follow the instructions of staff

- dress in accordance with the school dress code

- follow school rules and procedures

- be punctual and prepared for class

- respect others and their property

- behave in a manner that does not disrupt the learning of others

- behave in a manner that ensures a caring, safe and clean environment

Rights and responsibilities – version 1

All members of the school community have the:

Right

- to be treated with courtesy and respect

- to work in and enjoy a safe, secure and clean environment

- to teach and learn without disruption

- to achieve their educational potential

- to have their property respected

- to be proud of their achievements

Responsibility

- to show respect and courtesy to others

- to keep our environment safe, secure and clean

- to ensure that there is no disruption to another person's teaching–learning environment

- to develop their potential and to assist others in doing the same

- to respect student, staff and school property

- to ensure that their actions do not discredit the school

RULES AND CONSEQUENCES

DIMENSION 4

Rights and responsibilities – version 2

All members of the school community have rights and responsibilities.

Students have the right to:

- be treated with courtesy and respect
- work in a clean, safe environment
- learn without disruption
- achieve their potential
- have their property respected
- be proud of their achievements

Students have the responsibility to:

- follow teachers' instructions
- treat others with courtesy and respect
- contribute to a clean, safe environment
- ensure there is no disruption to the learning environment
- respect the property of others
- participate fully in their educational program
- ensure their actions do not discredit the school

Parents have the right to:

- be treated with courtesy and respect
- be informed about their child's progress
- expect their child to participate fully in his/her educational program
- have a forum to voice their opinion on school related matters

Parents have the responsibility to:

- treat others with courtesy and respect
- ensure that their child attends school
- ensure that their child has appropriate materials needed for learning
- monitor their child's progress
- be supportive of the school

Staff have the right to:

- be treated with courtesy and respect
- work in a clean, safe environment
- teach without disruption
- be supported by the whole school community

Staff have the responsibility to:

- treat others with courtesy and respect
- ensure the school environment is safe
- ensure good organisation and planning
- provide relevant and challenging educational programs
- support the school's ethos, policies and procedures

RULES AND CONSEQUENCES

DIMENSION 4

School rules

School compliance:

- Students must follow the instructions of staff.

School uniforms:

- Students are to dress in accordance with the school uniform code.

Designated student access areas:

- Students are only permitted in designated areas of the school.
- Students are only allowed in classrooms when a staff member is present.
- Students are not to use A or B Block centre areas as a thoroughfare.
- The following areas are out of bounds to all students:
  - bush land or gardens
  - car parks and roadways
  - area behind canteen
  - rear verandas of change rooms and D block
  - southern side of athletics track on oval
  - bush land on the edge of the oval.
- See out of bounds map for more details.
- Students are not permitted on school grounds after school or on weekends unless they are involved in some official organised activity.

Students out of class during lessons:

- Students out of class during lesson time must carry a student movement pass.

Leaving the school grounds:

- Students may only leave the school grounds during the school day after obtaining a permission note from the front office.

Bicycles:

- Students bringing bicycles to school must:
  - use bike paths to enter and leave the school,
  - place bicycles in enclosure before school,
  - walk with their bicycles on school grounds.

Skateboards:

- Skateboards are not to be ridden on school grounds at any time and should be left in the skateboard rack during school hours.

Unacceptable behaviour:

The following behaviours are not acceptable at school:

- Spitting
- Obscene language or swearing
- Verbal or physical abuse of others, harassment or fighting
- Throwing dangerous objects
- Splashing, squirting, water bombs or wetting other students
- Rough or dangerous games such as brandy or killer ball
- Running on verandahs or walkways
- Sitting or swinging on verandah rails or goals on oval
- Inappropriate physical displays of affection between students

Drugs and illicit substances:

- The use or possession of alcohol, tobacco, illegal drugs or illicit substances by students will not be tolerated at this school and strong consequences will apply.
- Students in possession of tobacco, alcohol, illegal drugs, illicit substances or any items associated with their use such as matches, lighters, cigarette papers, pipes or bongs, or who are under the influence of any unauthorised substances, are committing an offence and will face consequences.
- Students in the company of others using alcohol, tobacco, illegal drugs or illicit substances are also committing an offence and will face consequences.
- Trading, supplying or selling of any drugs, including medication such as ADD tablets or dexamphetamines, is considered a very serious offence and the police will be notified.
- Tobacco, alcohol or other drug emblems, slogans or logos are not permitted on clothing or jewellery worn to school. See school uniform code.

Other items not permitted at school:

- Chewing gum
- Electronic equipment such as portable CD or tape players and computer games
- Knives or weapons of any kind or any explosive device
- Laser pointers

Food and drinks:

- At the canteen, students should queue up in their appropriate line. Saving places or pushing in is not permitted.
- At lunchtime, students are to eat their lunch in their designated area, and remain seated until dismissed by the duty teacher.
- Food and drinks must not be taken past the yellow lines.

School buses:

- Normal school rules apply on school buses.

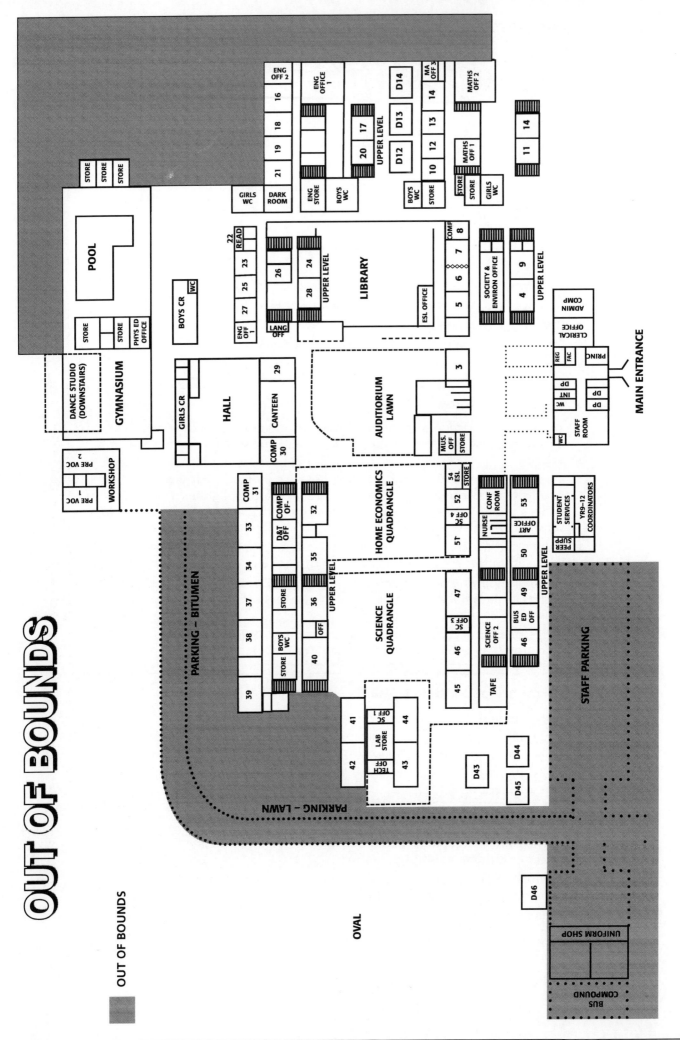

School uniform code

The correct uniform for day wear is:

Shirts: Sky blue polo shirt (short or long sleeve), plain or with school logo

Shorts: Navy knit shorts, NO logo or stripes
Navy dress shorts, NOT more than 13 cm above knee

Pants: Navy parasilk trackpants, NO logos or stripes
Navy fleecy trackpants
Navy plain girls slacks
Navy plain boys trousers

Skirts: Navy, pleated or 'A' line.

Tops: Navy fleecy jumper, plain or with school logo
School rugby top

Students are required to change for physical education and sports lessons. They will change back to normal uniform for general school classes.

The physical education and sport uniform is:

Shirts: gold polo shirt, plain or with school logo

Shorts: Royal blue knit shorts

Skirts: Royal blue sports skirt

Footwear: Suitable footwear should be worn – heavy soled boots such as Doc Marten's are not appropriate.

During physical education, certain items of jewellery are a potential source of injury to the wearer or to other students. These items must be removed. If this is not possible, they must be taped.

Notes

- Hats are strongly recommended for all students. For primary students, a policy of 'NO HAT – NO PLAY' applies during Terms 1 and 4.
- Hats are not to be worn in class.
- Denim jeans, leggings, board shorts or baggies, check jackets or shirts, thongs and exercise sandals are not acceptable.
- If jackets and overcoats need to be worn to school, they should be navy blue and should be taken off in class.
- T-shirts worn under school uniform should be sky blue, navy or white and only show at the neck (i.e. no long sleeves, or hanging out under shirts or jumpers).
- Gold sports shirts are not to be worn in class.
- Parents are strongly advised to place student names on all items of clothing.
- Students should not wear excessive jewellery or make-up.
- Clothing or jewellery with alcohol or drug logos, emblems or slogans are not permitted (e.g. cannabis leaf or 'bong' logo). This includes free dress days.

Jewellery, accessories and make-up code

All members of the school community have a responsibility to be well presented and to ensure that their presentation and actions do not discredit the school or compromise the health and safety of themselves or other students and staff.

Students are expected to follow teachers' requests with regard to the removal of make-up and jewellery if they do not meet the stated code of behaviour. Envelopes will be provided for any unacceptable items that students are asked to remove. These will be available for collection from the front office at the end of the school day. If accessories or jewellery become an object of distraction, they will be confiscated. Any logos relating to illegal substances or alcohol are not acceptable.

At times the students may be engaged in school activities that allow for the suspension of this policy.

Item	Acceptable	Not Acceptable
Make-up	Natural colours	Glitter, bright or unnatural colours
Nail polish	Natural, clear or light colours	Bright or unnatural colours
Hair colour	Natural tints, streaks and colours	Bright, vibrant, unnatural colours
Hairstyles		Bizarre and unconventional
Tattoos and stick-ons		Not acceptable if visible
Earrings	Studs and sleepers are preferred. Maximum of 2 earrings per ear.	Large, unsafe
Rings	Maximum of 2 rings – unobtrusive in size and style	Toe rings if visible
Body piercings	Only acceptable if not visible or in stud form	Hoops, rings and chains if visible
Bracelets	1 maximum (medical bracelets do not constitute jewellery)	Inappropriate sizes, materials, colours and multiple
Anklets		Not acceptable if visible
Watches	Acceptable if safe and encouraged to be worn	
Necklaces	1 maximum, multiple, multi-coloured	Oversized, dog collars, chokers
Hair accessories	Hairclips, scrunchies, bands, subtle and appropriate styles	Hairpieces, feathers, beads
Wallet and key accessories	Short clip on key and wallet rings	Chain
Sunglasses	Worn outside	Worn inside rooms or on top of the head when inside rooms
Offensive graffiti on clothes, books, bags, body or shoes		Strictly forbidden

Bullying and harassment

All members of the school community have the right to be treated with courtesy and respect. The following behaviours are NOT acceptable at school and are considered harassment.

Teasing, name calling or put-downs

Verbal threats

Threatening with objects

Nasty looks, signs or gestures

Property damaged or taken

Following

Physical contact

Spreading rumours

Spitting at or around others

Writing insults, graffiti or notes

Sexual comments or harassment

Racist comments

If you are being harassed, tell a teacher, don't put up with it!

If you are guilty of harassment, STOP!

Students who continued to harass others will be issued a harassment notice and face consequences and counselling!

Positive behaviour

Students can receive credit slips for positive behaviour.

 Each credit slip a student receives will be put into a 'lucky draw'. This will be drawn regularly by the home room teacher.

 Students will be awarded a Bronze Certificate for accumulating 20 credit slips in one year, and a Silver Certificate for accumulating 40.

 Any student who earns 60 credit slips in one year will be presented with a medallion – Gold Award.

 Students who have no lunch detentions or higher consequence at the end of term—i.e. those in 'good standing'—will automatically be invited to the end of term reward.

RULES AND CONSEQUENCES

Negative behaviour

Students can receive demerits for negative behaviour.

Students 'not taking responsibility' may be given

LEVEL ONE DEMERITS

3 level one demerits = community service

Students who are 'not behaving responsibly' may be given

LEVEL TWO DEMERITS

3 level two demerits = lunch detention

Students who show an inappropriate attitude towards teachers
or other students have committed a 'serious offence' and may be given a

LEVEL THREE DEMERIT

They will be sent to the deputy and may be given one of the following consequences: lunch detention, after-school detention, in-school suspension or an out-of-school suspension.

Students who continually disrupt a lesson may be **WITHDRAWN** from that class.

Students who receive three or more lunch detentions in one term will be referred to the deputy
and can expect the following consequences:

3 lunch detentions = 1 day class withdrawal
4 or more lunch detentions = extended class withdrawal

ATTENDANCE AT SPECIAL EVENTS SUCH AS THE END OF TERM REWARD AND SOCIALS

- All students start off the beginning of term in 'good standing'.
- Students who get a lunch detention or higher consequence lose their good standing.
- Only students in good standing will be invited to special events such as end of term rewards or socials.
- Students who have shown an improvement in behaviour, and have fewer than three consequences (not including community service), may apply to their home room teacher to reinstate their good standing. This application must also be approved by the relevant deputy or school leader.

ATTENDANCE AT SIGNIFICANT EXTRACURRICULAR EVENTS
e.g. camps and graduation

If a home room teacher considers a student has accumulated an unacceptable number of consequences throughout the year, he/she will refer the student to the principal, who will issue the student with a 'principal's caution'. This caution puts the student on notice that further misbehaviour will lead to his or her exclusion from a particular event such as a camp, the school ball/dinner or graduation.

Assembly code

- Move with your home room teacher quickly and quietly to your designated area.

- Wear full correct uniform.

- No jumpers tied around waists.

- Hats off.

- Sit upright and quietly at all times.

- Don't talk during assembly.

- Silence when a speaker stands behind the microphone.

- National Anthem
  - Rise and stand silently.
  - Stand with hands by your side.
  - Sing along.

- Applaud politely when appropriate.

- No whistling or inappropriate response; e.g. loud cheers, catcalls, jeering.

- No comments or noises when awards read out or when items announced.

- Respect the 'sense of occasion'; e.g. remembrance ceremonies.

- Award winners
  - Walk briskly.
  - Shake with right hand and receive with left hand, make eye contact with presenter.

- Don't stand up to leave until instructed by MC.

Guidelines for creating classroom rules

- They should be **consistent** with existing school rules.

- Try to **limit the number** of rules. There is no need to duplicate existing school rules.

- Allow **students to participate** in the formulation of rules if possible.

- Try to keep rules **positive**, although this is not always possible.

- Make them **clear** and not open to interpretation.

- **Display** rules prominently.

- Ensure that students know what the consequences of breaking the rules are.

- Review or add rules if necessary.

Rewards and Consequences

In Dimension 7 of this book I talk about the fact that people's behaviour is a reflection of their desire or need to meet their basic needs and, as Napoleon said; is driven by self interest (pleasure) or fear (pain). Individuals behave the way they do because they believe that this behaviour will:

- lead them towards pleasure (meeting their basic needs or reaching their goal of misbehaviour)
- lead them away from pain (discomfort or something they don't want to do)

We need to condition students into believing that behaving well will lead to pleasure. Rewards are one way that we can get students to associate good behaviour with pleasure.

We also need to condition students into believing that misbehaving will lead to pain (discomfort, loss of privileges, or something they don't want to do), so that they associate bad behaviour with pain. We need to make sure that our consequences are effective and are actually causing some discomfort to the student concerned.

The reward debate

Although I have mentioned that rewards are one way that we can get students to associate good behaviour with pleasure, there is some debate on the use of rewards.

Some practitioners argue that rewards are counter productive and undermine a student's intrinsic motivation. The most well known of

these people would be Alfie Kohn who wrote "Punished by Rewards". In my research, I have found studies that conclude rewards can undermine the intrinsic motivation of students and studies that do not. It appears that the effect depends on how the rewards are given. In her paper "Instructional Reinforcement", Kathleen Cotton's findings conclude that intrinsic motivation will not be undermined if:

- Rewards are relevant to the task.
- Rewards are perceived as a symbol of success rather than an attempt to control his or her behaviour.

She found that intrinsic motivation can be undermined if students are rewarded just for participating.

From this I would conclude that rewards are useful so long as they are in context and not seen as an effort to manipulate the students behaviour. People I deal with who work with very disruptive students use rewards as an integral part of their programs to help students modify their behaviour. My view is that you should do what works for you and sits well with your values. It is up to the individual to decide whether they give out rewards or not.

During my presentations I ask teachers what rewards they use in their classrooms. The following page lists ideas as suggested by both primary and high school teachers. Tick the box of any ideas which may be appropriate or useful for you.

Reward examples

Can be awarded for individuals, groups or faction

- ❏ Verbal comments – in public and/or private
- ❏ Credit slips
- ❏ Stickers
- ❏ Stamps
- ❏ Pens, pencils, rubbers, rulers etc.
- ❏ Lollies
- ❏ Chocolates
- ❏ Ice creams
- ❏ Cans of cool drink
- ❏ Chips
- ❏ Lucky dips
- ❏ McDonalds (or other fast food) lunch brought in
- ❏ McDonalds (or other) vouchers
- ❏ Visit principal or other school leader
- ❏ Help out in a lower grade class
- ❏ Merit certificates
- ❏ Extra computer time
- ❏ Extra sport time
- ❏ Free time pass
- ❏ Puzzles
- ❏ Magazines
- ❏ Badges
- ❏ $2 shop prizes
- ❏ Play music in class
- ❏ Watch video/DVD
- ❏ Play board games
- ❏ Note home – letter of commendation
- ❏ Tick/tally charts – keep track of students' positive behaviour. Prizes for reaching certain levels.
- ❏ Badges – students wear a name badge (conference type badge) and get little stickers to put on them. A reward is given when you get a certain number. Great for relief teachers.
- ❏ Raffle tickets – have a lucky draw at the end of the day or week.
- ❏ Tokens for individual, group, class or faction competitions
- ❏ Marble Jar – get a marble for doing some thing good. When the jar is full class gets a reward.

- ❏ Snakes and Ladders – students get to spin the dice for a continuous game of snakes and ladders. First person or group to finish gets a reward.
- ❏ Rocket to the Moon – each time a student does something good the rocket (which is suspended on a piece of string) moves forward 10 centimetres (or what ever). When it "gets to the moon" the class gets a reward.
- ❏ Passport – get a stamp for doing something good, fill the passport and get a trip to ... the canteen (or whatever).
- ❏ Chase the Ace – student get to draw a card from a pack of cards. If they draw an Ace, King, Queen or Jack they get a predetermined prize.
- ❏ Jag the Joker – similar to Chase the Ace, but if they draw a joker they get a special prize.
- ❏ Chocolate wheel – for those who are very organised. Students get to spin the wheel. Each number represents a different prize.
- ❏ Students get to play a game of checkers with 'ripe raspberries' lollies. When you take an opponent's 'piece' you get to eat it.
- ❏ Sporting stickers and cards – football cards etc.
- ❏ The canteen speciality
- ❏ Popcorn maker – students get to make popcorn and share it with the class.
- ❏ Smiley face stuff
- ❏ Reward tree – like a Christmas tree with little rewards stuck on them.
- ❏ Play money – students' get play money and bid for items at the end of week/month or term auction. You can get great items from $2 shops.
- ❏ Don't forget to ask your students what they would value as a reward.

RULES AND CONSEQUENCES

Consequences

Although students need to be accountable for their behaviour, 'tough consequences' alone are not the answer. Consequences serve to let students know that their behaviour is unacceptable, but along with consequences we need to have in place strategies to help offenders change their behaviour. For any consequence there should also be some process for students to repair the damage done and to be self-reflective about their behaviour in order to plan for improvement. You might call these 'corrective' or 'supportive' strategies. There are some useful ideas in Dimension 5 – Resources, and Dimension – 7 Rescue and support. See 'Examples of corrective and support strategies to supplement consequences', this below.

Consequence examples

Just as I ask participants in my seminars about what rewards they use, I ask them what consequences work for them. The answer is always the same. It depends on the student and it depends on the class. Below is a list of possible consequences given to me by practicing teachers. Tick the box of any that might be appropriate and useful for you.

❏ Move student to a different seat
❏ Isolation within class
❏ Demerit slip
❏ 'Chill Out' pass
❏ Lines
❏ Letter to parent
❏ Email parent
❏ Phone call to parent on the spot – get student to talk to them
❏ Phone call to parent after class
❏ SMS text message
❏ Apology letter
❏ Loss of privileges eg sport, computers
❏ Loss of privileges at home (with parent support)
❏ Community service

❏ Class withdrawal – admin, buddy class, time out room
❏ Lunch detention
❏ After school detention
❏ Saturday morning detention
❏ Weekend detention (with the support of the parent)
❏ Extended class withdrawal
❏ In school suspension
❏ Out of school suspension
❏ Time spent in out of hours counselling - in lieu of detention/suspension
❏ Restorative justice/shame management/restitution

Ask your students what consequences they think would be appropriate.

Examples of corrective and support strategies to supplement consequences

You can find the following corrective and support strategies in this book

❏ Restorative justice process (p. 84)
❏ Lunch detention self-reflection (p. 115)
❏ Class withdrawal 'Work It Out' sheet – version 1 (p. 117)
❏ 'Work It Out' sheet versions 2 (p. 118)
❏ Demerit lines (p. 129)
❏ Student apology note (p. 130)
❏ Teachers chill out pass (p. 131)
❏ Student services referral notice (p. 147)
❏ School reminders fridge magnet

(p. 149)
❏ Individual education/behaviour plan (p. 150)
❏ Student chill out pass (p. 149)
❏ Daily Progress report version 1 (pp. 152 – 153)
❏ Daily Progress report version 2 (p. 154)
❏ Daily goal report (p. 155)
❏ Behaviour and progress report (p. 156)
❏ Student contract (p. 157)
❏ Case conference record (p. 158)

Bullying and harassment policy – Example

Ref: Roleystone District High School Behaviour Management Plan

Our aim

We want students to develop respect for others and their rights. All students and teachers have the right to learn and work in an environment free from harassment and it is the responsibility of each of us to make sure this happens.

Harassment is any behaviour that is unwarranted, unwelcome and undesired that causes a person to feel discomfort. It is behaviour by one or more persons towards another which is designed to hurt, embarrass, upset or cause discomfort. Bullying is one form of harassment.

Some examples of harassment at school include:

- teasing and rumours
- unwarranted touching
- discrimination
- physical contact
- name calling
- threats
- bullying
- sexual harassment
- sending nasty notes
- racist comments
- damage or interference to property
- threatening or aggressive behaviour
- put-downs
- deliberately being left out of activities
- graffiti that is derogatory about another student

Are you a bully?

- Do you tease, abuse or hit others?
- Do you call people names?
- Do you insult, belittle or intimidate?
- Do you take part with a group in helping to insult and offend others?
- Do you condone bullying of others by laughing or by failing to intervene?

If **yes**, then STOP.

YOU CAN CONTROL WHAT HAPPENS

- Do not retaliate by physical or verbal harassment
- Simply knowing that you can do something about it makes a difference

So what can you do?

- Ignore it. Show that it does not upset you. The bully is then not encouraged and may stop.
- Confront the person harassing you. Tell him/her that his/her actions are unwanted or illegal.
- Talk it over openly with your friends, parents or teachers. They can help you make a decision

DEALING WITH HARASSMENT AT SCHOOL

Our school approach is initially one of 'no blame'.* This involves meetings between a staff member, the victim(s) and the person involved in the harassment. Feelings are discussed, and details of the incident are noted; however, blame is not attributed. Responsibility is placed in the hands of the group. However, if the harassment is severe enough, the offender(s) will face consequences as per the behaviour management plan.

* *'No blame' refers to students being involved in initial counselling but not necessarily being punished at this stage.*

First reported incident

- Harassment notice is sent to home room teacher, Year group leader or deputy (depending on the severity of the harassment), with details of the incident.
- Discussion and counselling (jointly and separately) of all parties involved.
- Action taken recorded on the harassment notice. One copy goes to the home room records file of the person(s) initiating the harassment, and the duplicate goes to the harassment records file at the front office.
- Demerit slip issued if appropriate.

The aim is to raise awareness

Second and further incidents

- Demerit slip issued and appropriate consequence given.
- Parent will be informed at this stage.
- Repeat victims and offenders may be referred to the school psychologist or student services team for counselling.

REPORTING HARASSMENT AT SCHOOL

You can report incidents of harassment to any person you feel comfortable talking to and who can help you deal with the harassment, such as:

A teacher, a Year leader, a deputy, the principal, chaplain or school psychologist.

WAYS YOU CAN STOP HARASSMENT

As a student:

- Gain an understanding of the policy.
- Respect the rights of all members of the community.
- Respect the rights of others to report incidents of harassment.
- Do not stand by and watch, get help.
- Show that you and your friends disapprove in an appropriate way.
- Give support to students who may be. harassed

- Be careful about teasing or personal remarks; imagine how you might feel.
- Recognise that the harassment will dealt with as part of the behaviour management plan

As a parent:

- Be aware of what harassment is:
- Be aware of the school's policy on harassment.
- Actively support the school's bullying and harassment policy.
- Freely discuss incidents of harassment with the school without prejudice.
- Encourage your child's self-esteem by being positive in the things you say and do.
- Encourage your child to report incidents of harassment.
- Model appropriate behaviour.

As a teacher:

- Make sure you understand the harassment policy and procedures.
- Actively discourage put-downs or other forms of harassment.
- Reinforce the policy at every opportunity.
- Model appropriate behaviour.
- Record incidents of harassment on a harassment notice.
- Support students who are dealing with harassment.

FUNMAN SAYS:

I used to have a tough time at school. I often got picked on and roughed up by big kids, but I especially hated it when they gave me big wedgies by pulling my pants up as high as they could. That's when I decided to give up teaching.

School dress code policy – example

After extensive consultation with all sectors of the school community, this school has established a dress code. The school decision making group believes that a dress code is necessary because it:

- gives students a sense of belonging,
- instils pride in the school,
- promotes a sense of equality among students,
- prepares students for the future as many work situations have dress and safety codes.

Availability of dress code Items:

The sale of uniforms, both new and secondhand, is a service provided by the Parents and Citizens association through its clothing pool. Items approved by the school council for the school dress code, as detailed on the clothing pool price list, are deemed to provide a sense of fashion, comfort and flexibility in dress which will encourage students to wear a uniform to school.

Modifications to dress code:

Students who, for religious or health reasons, may wish to modify the school dress code, should apply to the principal. Staff will be informed of any granted exemptions or modifications.

As students will be made aware of this policy on enrolment at this school, it is not expected that there will be many occasions of non-compliance. However, students not following dress code will receive:

- counselling from a designated staff member on the benefits and requirements of uniform,
- a pass for an agreed length of time for dress modification,
- parent contact.

Non-compliance with the dress code will be recorded by school administrators and, where exemption has not been sought, may result in a student being denied the opportunity to represent our school in music and sporting events or involvement in excursions and school functions.

Clothing not meeting the school dress code will be replaced by clean secondhand items. Students will borrow these items for that school day.

> **New and secondhand uniform items are available from the clothing pool every Friday 8.00 – 9.00 am (during term time).**

Consequences of smoking at school policy – Example

Smoking is not permitted at this school. For your information, the consequences for students smoking at this school are listed below. The first offence consequence is designed to have a positive health education outcome, but please note that the second and third offences indicate a deliberate and persistent lack of cooperation with the school and result in suspension.

SCHOOL RULE

Drugs and illicit substances

- The use or possession of alcohol, tobacco, illegal drugs or illicit substances by students will not be tolerated at this school and strong consequences will apply.

- Students in possession of tobacco, alcohol, illegal drugs, illicit substances or any items associated with their use, such as matches, lighters, cigarette papers, pipes or bongs, or who are under the influence of any unauthorised substances, are committing an offence and will face consequences.

- Students in the company of others using alcohol, tobacco, illegal drugs or illicit substances are also committing an offence and will face consequences.

- Trading, supplying or selling of any drugs, including medication such as ADD tablets or dexamphetamines, are considered very serious offences and the police will be notified.

- Tobacco, alcohol or other drug emblems, slogans or logos are not permitted on clothing or jewellery worn to school.

First offence:

Counselling – to follow the viewing of a video on smoking. Completion, in student's own time, of an assignment testing factual knowledge and personal opinions of the harmful effects of smoking. Strong warning on consequences of further offences. Parents will be notified.

Second offence:

Two (2) days' suspension from school. Letter and telephone call to parents.

Subsequent offences:

Four (4) days' suspension from school at the discretion of the principal. Letter and telephone call to parents.

NOTE:

- Students caught smoking at interschool functions will be banned from further participation in such functions for the remainder of the term at least.

- Any smoking offence could lead to loss of privileges such as attendance at a school camp.

- Refusal to cooperate or take seriously any consequence will lead to the student moving to the next consequence at the discretion of the principal.

- The suspension referred to in the second and subsequent offences is suspension from school and is recorded on school records and could affect future employment prospects. If a total of 30 days or more is accumulated, the student must attend an exclusion panel which may result in the termination of future attendance at all state schools.

Consequences of drug-related offences (other than smoking) – Example

The use or possession of alcohol, tobacco, illegal drugs, illicit substances or associated implements by students will not be tolerated at this school.

Unauthorised drug use by students at this school will result in the following action:

- Parent(s) will be contacted and an interview time arranged to suit the school's administration and the parent(s).
- The student will be suspended from school for a period of 4–10 days for a first offence.
- If a subsequent instance of unauthorised drug use occurs, the student will receive the maximum suspension period of 10 days, and be recommended for exclusion.
- Any offence involving drug use or possession may be reported to the police.

- A second or subsequent offence will automatically be reported to the police and action will be taken which they deem appropriate.
- Any offence involving the supply of unauthorised drugs will also be reported to the police.
- The student will be required to attend counselling sessions.
- The school staff will be given all appropriate information on incident.
- On return to school from suspension, the student will report immediately to the appropriate member of the administration and complete a contract specifically dealing with illicit drug use.
- The student's behaviour and progress will be monitored by all staff.

Exclusion of students from significant extracurricular activities policy – Example

NOTE: Local education authority regulations need to be checked before finalising this document.

Preamble

This policy is based on the following:

- Involvement of students in *significant extracurricular activities which have been organised by the school is a privilege which must be earnt. It is not a right.

- The school has a right to invite students to participate in significant extracurricular activities.

- Students who disregard the rules of the school by behaving unacceptably will jeopardise their chances of being invited to participate in significant extracurricular activities.

- The principal reserves the right to issue students with a **formal caution. A breach of the conditions of a caution could preclude a student from a significant extracurricular activity.

Policy

- Student behaviour will be monitored by all teaching and administrative staff through the school behaviour management system. Documentation should be thorough and complete.

- Home room teachers will work closely with Year leaders (where relevant) and deputy principals to identify students who are at risk of not being invited to significant extracurricular activities.

- Teachers, Year leaders or deputies will inform the principal of students who are at risk of not being invited to significant extracurricular activities.

- At a time deemed appropriate by Year leaders and deputies, the principal will interview students who are at risk of not being invited to a significant extracurricular activity. A letter will be sent home to parents.

- A formal caution will be issued by the principal to the student.

- This will be known as the 'Principal's caution'

- Copies will be provided for form teachers, Year leaders, deputies and parents.

- Year leaders and deputies will inform the principal of continuing unacceptable behaviour of students who have been issued with a formal caution.

- The principal will inform parents when a student is in breach of a caution. The principal will also inform parents if this behaviour excludes their child from a significant extracurricular activity. This will be done in full collaboration with Year leaders, deputies and form teachers.

---

* Defined as activities which enrich the school experience of children. They may include camps, school ball/dinner dance or graduation functions.

** Defined as the point of intervention by the principal. A caution serves notice to a student that further unacceptable behaviour reported to the principal could exclude them from camps and/or graduation functions.

PLEASE NOTE

Students who have been found guilty of supplying or using an illicit drug in the school will be excluded from all extracurricular activities for that year.

Restorative justice and restitution

For those who commit serious offences or continuously misbehave

Students who commit serious offences or continuously misbehave need to be accountable for their behaviour. This is why we have consequences. However, those who have administered the toughest consequences a school can issue would agree – for some students the toughest consequence will not stop them offending. Along with consequences we need strategies to help them change their behaviour. We need a process that helps them recognise the harm they have done and how their behaviour affects the people around them. It should also focus on how they might go about repairing the damage and improve their behaviour. A restorative justice process aims to do just this.

Restorative justice practices have been successfully used in the juvenile justice system for a number of years and aim to repair and rebuild relationships. They involve a series of interventions designed to resolve serious incidents of harm. Some of these strategies include conferencing, 'circlespeak' and victim-offender mediation. The aim of the process is to get all parties concerned back into the community as responsible and resilient members.

Restorative justice involves building a support system around individuals who have offended, as they work through a restitution process. A 'community of support' is created, made up of those people who respect and care most about the victim(s) and the offender(s). It might include parents, relatives, friends, teachers or a chaplain. By using 'communities of support' in the process, offenders are held accountable for their actions in a supportive environment.

The process involves an element of shame management with a confrontation between the victim and the offender. In a forum that heavily supports the offender, he/she acknowledges the harm that has been done and determines how to make amends. It must be made quite clear that the behaviour is not condoned, but he/she does have the support of the community. It is also most important that the offender can 'discharge the shame' through the process. If the shame remains with the person it will have a negative effective.

The emphasis of the restorative justice process in on the fact that the offender has violated the school community and harmed people and relationships – as opposed to breaking school rules. It is about finding solutions to the problems, not about fixing blame. It provides an opportunity for the offender to realise the physical, emotional and social damage he/she has caused and how best to seek to make amends.

In her article *Bullying and victimisation in schools: A restorative justice approach*, Morrison outlines five basic principles or beliefs that underpin an effective restorative justice program.

- A belief that offenders and victims are able to change their behaviour.

- Offenders should not be put-down or denigrated in the process.

- The offender must acknowledge that he/she has caused harm to others.

- There must be some kind of restitution or reparation for the harm that has been done.

- The 'community of support' treats both the victim and the offender as valued members of the school community throughout the process.

Restorative justice and restitution – A sample process

There are a variety of strategies that could be used, but a typical process might go as follows.

Facilitation

A facilitator is appointed who makes sure the five principles (see p. 84) are adhered to throughout the process. A conference is convened with a 'community of support' group. The facilitator makes it clear that the process is about finding solutions to the problems, not about fixing the blame.

Community of support

A 'community of support' is made up of those people who respect and care most about the victim(s) and the offender(s) and might include parents, relatives, friends, teachers, the deputy or the chaplain.

Support

The facilitator explains to the offender that the 'community of support' is there to support him/her throughout the process.

How the behaviour has affected others

The group challenges the offender to consider how his/her behaviour has affected others.

Circlespeak

Members of the 'community of support' speak in turn, giving their account of how the incident(s) have affected them.

Making amends

It is important that the offender is clear that this part of the process is about restitution, not punishment.

Facilitator to the offender

This has happened, what can you do to fix it? The restitution should be related to the offence where possible.

The plan

What plan can you put in place to repair the damage and compensate the people who have been wronged? How can we help you do this?

Follow up

The facilitator should schedule follow-up meetings with the victim and the offender to monitor progress.

Many schools and juvenile justice systems have reported excellent results in modifying behaviour using this restorative justice approach. Others have been less successful. If the process is to be effective it is most important that the five principles are adhered to. The offender needs to feel supported throughout the process, he/she needs to acknowledge the harm that has been caused, and the restitution that is made needs to be acceptable to all parties.

ROUTINES AND ROLES

Procedures, roles and responsibilities for implementing the behaviour management plan

In this section:

Operational procedures ◄

Roles and responsibilities ◄

ROUTINES AND ROLES

A sample behaviour management plan

NOTE: Documents mentioned in this sample plan can be found in other sections of this book.

SCHOOL VISION

'A school community where individuals seek academic, creative and physical excellence to achieve their potential with respect and responsibility towards themselves, others and the environment.'

The behaviour management plan aims to address this vision with the following aims:

AIMS

Our behaviour management plan aims to:

- develop a caring, safe and positive school environment that encourages a strong sense of belonging and where the rights and responsibilities of individuals are recognised and respected
- foster positive relationships between members of the school community
- develop a clear set of rules, policies and procedures that protect the rights of individuals and resolve conflict in a positive manner

- make students accountable for their own behaviour, and to implement fair but effective consequences for misbehaviour which encourage students to recognise the rights of others and to be aware of their own responsibilities
- provide a support services infrastructure to assist students who are having behavioural or other problems
- provide a support services infrastructure to support staff in managing student behaviour and in other areas of need
- develop strong links with parents to keep them informed of their child's progress

GUIDELINES OF BEHAVIOUR

SCHOOL CODE OF BEHAVIOUR

It is expected that members of the school community will show:

CARE
- for others
- for the school environment

RESPECT
- for others and their property
- for school rules

COURTESY
- by acknowledging others
- by speaking politely
- by using good manners

RESPONSIBILITY
- by acknowledging others
- by speaking politely
- by using good manners

This code of behaviour acts as an overarching guide for behaviour in this school. For further clarification, the school community has developed a set of guidelines which provide clearer details of expected student behaviour. They are outlined in the following school codes, which are either displayed around the school or easily accessed. (See Dimension 4, Rules – for school code documents.)

- School code wheel
- Code of behaviour
- Rights and responsibilities
- School rules
- Out of bounds map
- School uniform code
- Jewellery, accessories and make-up code
- Bullying and harassment
- Appreciation of positive behaviour
- Consequences of negative behaviour
- Assembly code
- Classroom rules (these vary from class to class)

These documents provide clear guidelines of expected student behaviour, and include consequences for students who choose not to follow them. Students should be directed to view the relevant document if their behaviour is outside these guidelines.

INTERVENTION POINTS

The **behaviour management plan** also has a series of **intervention points**. When a student reaches certain consequences for negative behaviour, various strategies are implemented to try to help the student change this behaviour. Some of these strategies may include letters or phone calls to parents, referrals to the student services team for counselling or life skills courses, parent interviews or case conferences.

POSITIVE BEHAVIOUR

Teachers seeing students displaying positive behaviour may reward them with a credit slip (printed in duplicate). One copy is given to the student and the other is given to or kept by the home room teacher who records

it. Accumulation of credit slips leads to other rewards throughout the year:

- Each credit slip a student receives is put into a lucky draw. This is drawn regularly by his or her home room teacher.
- If a student earns 20 credit slips, he/she will receive a bronze certificate and for 40 a silver certificate. Both will be presented at an assembly.
- Any student who earns 60 credit slips in one year will be presented with a medallion (gold award).
- Students who have no detentions, suspensions or other serious consequences at the end of term are said to be in 'good standing' and will be invited to the end of term reward and other events such as socials.
- Students who lose their good standing can apply to their home room teacher to have it reinstated if they have shown a pattern of improved behaviour. This must be approved by the appropriate deputy or Year leader.
- Parents are encouraged to reinforce the credit slip system at home.

NEGATIVE BEHAVIOUR

Negative behaviour is broken into three levels:

Level one – Not taking responsibility

These are minor offences such as lateness, diary not signed or brought to class, incorrect uniform, equipment not brought to class, homework not done or food taken to 'out of bounds' areas.

Level two – Not behaving responsibly

These include offences such as disturbing other students, interrupting teacher, failing to follow teacher instructions, not completing class work, rough play or swearing.

Level three – Serious offences

These include offences such as disobeying a teacher, insolent behaviour, significant disruption of a lesson, vandalism, violence, fighting, throwing dangerous objects,

unauthorised drug use, stealing, interfering with another person's property, using abusive language or gestures towards others.

If students display negative behaviour they can be issued with a demerit slip. Demerit slips should only be issued as a last resort or for significant inappropriate behaviour.

Level one offence procedures and consequences

Teachers may issue a *level one demerit slip* (printed in duplicate) for any of these offences. They may be given 1, 2, or 3 demerits depending on the severity of the offence. These slips are kept by or given to the home room teacher who records them and questions the student regarding the incident.

Students do not get a copy of the *demerit slip*.

Consequences are designed to promote responsible behaviour.

Students who accumulate three *level one demerits* in one term* will be given a 15-minute **COMMUNITY SERVICE** task to do. (*some schools might find it more appropriate to issue consequences when demerits are accumulated over shorter periods; e.g. five weeks, one week, one day). These may include things such as cleaning desks, tidying shelves, counting books or yard duty. Parents will be notified by the home room teacher via the student diary if their child is given a **COMMUNITY SERVICE**. Students should also bring home a community service notice for parents to sign to acknowledge that they are aware of their child reaching that consequence. The student returns the signed notice to the home room teacher for filing.

Intervention point – Students who accumulate **3 COMMUNITY SERVICES** in one term should be referred to the student services team, and parents should be contacted by the home room teacher through either a letter of concern or a phone call.

Intervention point – If a student gets 4 or more **COMMUNITY SERVICES** in one term, a parent interview should be requested by the home room teacher.

Level two offence procedures and consequences

Level two – Not behaving responsibly – these include offences such as disturbing other students, interrupting teacher, failing to following teacher instructions, not completing class work, rough play or swearing.

Teachers may issue a *level two demerit slip* for any of these offences. They may be given 1, 2, or 3 demerits depending on the severity of the offence. These slips are kept by or given to the home room teacher who records them and questions the student regarding the incident. Students do not get a copy of the demerit slip.

Consequences are designed to allow students to reflect on their behaviour and plan for improvement.

Students who accumulate three *level two demerits* in one term will be given a **LUNCH DETENTION**. During lunch detentions, students fill out a self-reflection sheet on the back of the lunch detention notice. Parents will be notified by the home room teacher via the student diary if their child is given a **LUNCH DETENTION**. Students should also bring home the lunch detention notice for parents to sign to acknowledge that they are aware of their child reaching that consequence. The student returns the signed notice to the home room teacher for filing.

Students who accumulate 3 or more **LUNCH DETENTIONS** in one term* face further consequences: (*some schools might find it more appropriate to issue consequences when demerits are accumulated over shorter periods; e.g. five weeks, one week, one day)

- 3 **LUNCH DETENTIONS** = 1 day **CLASS WITHDRAWAL**
- 4 or more **LUNCH DETENTIONS** = **EXTENDED CLASS WITHDRAWAL**
- Students who are given a **LUNCH DETENTION, CLASS WITHDRAWAL,** an **IN-SCHOOL** or **OUT-OF-SCHOOL SUSPENSION,** (or other serious consequences) lose their good standing and will not be automatically invited to the end of term reward or socials. Students can apply to have their good standing reinstated.

Students who are continually disruptive in one class may be withdrawn from that class to work with another class or in the time out room – **CLASS WITHDRAWAL**.

Students who show a pattern of continual disruption may be withdrawn from all classes for a period of time on an **EXTENDED CLASS WITHDRAWAL**.

Intervention point – Students who accumulate 3 **LUNCH DETENTIONS** in one term, should be referred to the student services team, and parents should be contacted by the home room teacher through either a letter of concern or a phone call.

Intervention point – If a student gets 4 or more **LUNCH DETENTIONS** in one term, a parent interview should be requested by the home room teacher.

Level three offence procedures and Consequences

Level three – Serious offences

These include offences such as disobeying a teacher, insolent behaviour, significant disruption of a lesson, vandalism, violence, fighting, throwing dangerous objects, unauthorised drug use, stealing, interfering with another person's property, using abusive language or gestures towards others.

Consequences are designed to demonstrate that students will lose privileges if they don't respect the rights of others.

Teachers will issue a *level three demerit slip* for any of these offences and the student will be sent to the appropriate deputy. One copy of the demerit slip is sent to the deputy and the other copy is kept by or given to the home room teacher for recording. Students **do not** get a copy of the demerit slip.

The deputy concerned, or the principal, will determine the consequences for students who commit *level three offences.* These consequences may include **LUNCH DETENTION, AFTER-SCHOOL DETENTION, IN-SCHOOL SUSPENSION,** or an **OUT-OF-SCHOOL SUSPENSION**, depending on the severity of the offence.

Intervention point – Parents will be notified by the deputy. The student may also be referred for counselling, depending on the nature of the offence.

The deputy will also notify the home room teacher of the consequence with a detention/suspension notice which gets filed by teacher.

Intervention point – For students who accumulate 10 or more days' suspension (in-school or out-of-school) in one year, a **CASE CONFERENCE** should be convened.

BULLYING AND HARASSMENT

(See also separate *bullying and harassment policy*)

Harassment or bullying will not be tolerated at this school. Harassment can include incidents such as teasing, name calling or put-downs, verbal threats, nasty looks, signs or gestures, property taken or damaged, following, physical contact, spreading rumours, spitting at or around others, writing insults, graffiti or notes, sexual or racist comments.

Depending on the severity of the harassment, the school approach is initially one of 'no blame' and counselling. This is in order to try and solve the problem, and so that the victim is not harassed further because of sanctions given to the offender. However, if it is warranted, the offender will also face consequences as per the behaviour management plan.

Bullying or harassment procedures and consequences

Incidents of harassment are recorded on a harassment notice (printed in duplicate) and kept by or given to the home room teacher who will refer it to the Year leader or deputy if appropriate, depending on the severity of the harassment. Demerit slips are also issued to the offenders only if appropriate. The home room teacher, Year leader or deputy then convenes a meeting of all persons involved in the harassment to have discussion and counselling, in order to try and resolve the problem. The action taken is then recorded

on the harassment notice. One copy goes to the offender(s) home room teacher for filing, the other copy goes to the harassment records file at the front office, in order to keep documentation of what was done about the incident.

Intervention point – In the event of serious offences, parents or police should be notified.

Second and further incidents

Harassment notice and demerit slips given, depending on the incident.

Intervention point – Parents of victims and offenders notified.

Intervention point – Repeat victims and offenders should be referred to the student services team.

GOOD STANDING

- All students start off the term in 'good standing'.
- Students who incur a **LUNCH** or **AFTER SCHOOL DETENTION**, an **IN-SCHOOL** or **OUT-OF-SCHOOL SUSPENSION**, or any serious consequences lose their 'good standing' and will not be automatically invited to the end of term reward or socials.
- Students may apply to their home room teacher to have their good standing reinstated. The home room teacher may approve this if the student has shown a pattern of improved behaviour.
- The application must also be approved by the appropriate deputy or Year leader.
- The application process should culminate in the student visiting the deputy's office with his/her application for final approval.

PRINCIPAL'S CAUTION – SIGNIFICANT EXTRACURRICULAR EVENTS

- Students who accumulate an unacceptable number of consequences throughout the year may be given a 'principal's caution'. Any unacceptable

behaviour after this caution may exclude them from significant extracurricular events such as camps, excursions or the school ball.

SUMMARY OF INTERVENTION POINTS

The behaviour management plan has a series of intervention points.

When a student reaches certain consequences for negative behaviour, various intervention methods are implemented to try to change this behaviour.

At these intervention points, the following procedures may be used:

- letters of concern or phone calls to parents
- referrals to the student services team for counselling or specialised courses
- parent interviews
- case conferences
- referrals to the police (in the case of incidents involving drugs or other serious offences)

Below is a list of intervention points.

3 COMMUNITY SERVICES
- Letter of concern or phone call to parent plus
- Student services referral.

4 COMMUNITY SERVICES
- Parent interview requested.
- 'School reminders' fridge magnet sent home.

3 LUNCH DETENTIONS
- Letter of concern or phone call to parent plus
- Student services referral.

4 LUNCH DETENTIONS
- Parent interview requested.

2 HARASSMENT NOTICES
- Parent should be contacted by home room teacher.

CLASS WITHDRAWAL
- Parent should be contacted by home room teacher.

LEVEL THREE CONSEQUENCES
- Deputy contacts parents if appropriate.

10 DAYS ACCUMULATED SUSPENSION (in or out of school – in one year)

Deputy convenes a case conference with student, parent/s, school psychologist, home room teacher, principal or deputy and a representative from the local education authority.

INCIDENTS INVOLVING DRUGS OR OTHER SERIOUS OFFENCES

Deputy may refer student(s) to the police service for counselling or legal consequences.

Although these procedures are put into practice after reaching these intervention points, any student who is considered 'at risk', (e.g. behaviourally, socially or academically), can be referred to the student services team, and/or parents can be contacted at any time.

REVIEW

The effectiveness of this behaviour management plan is monitored throughout the year. It is to be reviewed annually at a special BMIS committee meeting late in term three of each year.

FUNMAN SAYS:

'Young Johnny won't be coming to school today as he is sick', said the voice on the telephone.

'Is that you, Johnny?' said the principal.

'No, it's my dad.'

Procedures for managing classroom behaviour

Each teacher has his or her own style of classroom management and the year level of the students should be taken into account. However, in the interests of a consistent and fair behaviour management plan, staff should use the following steps as a guideline.

STEP 1 **Tactical ignoring**

- Tactically ignore those who are doing the wrong thing (e.g. yelling out) and respond to those who do the right thing (e.g. have their hand up).

STEP 2 **Proximity praise/reward**

- Where a student is misbehaving, praise another student close by who is doing the 'right thing'.
- Catch the student doing something good – praise him/her.
- Check if the student is coping with the task.
- Ask the student why he or she is misbehaving.

STEP 3 **Rule reminder**

- Refer student to displayed rules.

STEP 4 **Warning – verbal reprimand**

- State the problem and clearly state the required behaviour.
- Be assertive and use 'I' statements; e.g. 'I don't want you to throw paper in the room, and if you do it again you will be choosing to get a consequence'.
- Write name on classroom behaviour chart or fill in name on demerit slip.
- Use a 'chill out pass'

STEP 5 **Issue the consequence**

- Loss of privilege; e.g. games, sport, use of computers.

Or Go to step 4a, 4b, or 4c depending on the nature of the misbehaviour.

Step 4a – Issue level two demerit

- Write X on classroom behaviour chart next to student's name – student gets 1 level two demerit.

Step 4b – isolate within classroom

- Write XX on classroom behaviour chart next to student's name – student gets another level two demerit.

Step 4c – class withdrawal

Send to support teacher with class withdrawal notice or send to deputy with demerit slip – student gets a third level two demerit (i.e. lunch detention). Deputy may put student in time-out room.

CLASSROOM BEHAVIOUR CHART

Name	Rule reminder	Warning 1 demerit	Isolation 2 demerits THINK SPOT	Withdrawal 3 demerits DETENTION

Alternative action

Chill-out pass | Class withdrawal

MANAGING STUDENT BEHAVIOUR – FLOW CHART

CLASSROOM

LEVEL ONE	LEVEL TWO	LEVEL THREE
Not taking responsibility	Not behaving responsibly	Serious offences
Issue **LEVEL ONE** demerit slip	Name on board or fill in name in demerit slip –	Issue **LEVEL THREE** demerit slip
Form teacher action	**WARNING**	SEND STUDENT TO DEPUTY
	First X = 1 LEVEL TWO DEMERIT	Deputy action
	Second X = 2 LEVEL TWO DEMERITS **ISOLATED WITHIN CLASSROOM**	
	Third X = 3 LEVEL TWO DEMERITS **CLASS WITHDRAWAL**	

for continual disruption
Issue support teacher referral notice
SEND STUDENT TO SUPPORT TEACHER
Form teacher action

for serious offences
Issue LEVEL THREE demerit slip
SEND STUDENT TO DEPUTY
Deputy action

Examples of NOT TAKING RESPONSIBILITY

- Late to class
- Not having correct equipment
- Food past yellow line
- Homework not completed
- No diary/not signed
- Incorrect school uniform

HARASSMENT

Any incidents of harassment/ bullying in the classroom or in the school yard should be referred to either the offending student/s

Form teacher

Year coordinator/team leader

or

School psychologist

Deputy

depending on the severity of the harassment

on a HARASSMENT NOTICE

in order to resolve the problem and prevent further conflict

Examples of NOT BEHAVING RESPONSIBLY

- Disturbing other students
- Not completing class work
- Failing to follow teacher instructions
- Swearing
- Interrupting teacher
- Rough play

SCHOOLYARD

LEVEL ONE	LEVEL TWO	LEVEL THREE
Not taking responsibility	Not behaving responsibly	Serious offences
Issue **LEVEL ONE** demerit slip	Issue **LEVEL TWO** demerit slip	Issue **LEVEL THREE** demerit slip
Form teacher action	Form teacher action	SEND STUDENT TO DEPUTY
		Deputy action

Examples of SERIOUS OFFENCES

- Vandalising property
- Violence (fight, push, trip, hit)
- Disobeying teacher
- Using abusive language or gestures
- Throwing objects
- Stealing

Behaviour management toolkit   www.ricgroup.com.au   R.I.C. Publications

Procedures for managing schoolyard behaviour

- The duty teachers are responsible for the safety and acceptable behaviour of students in the areas they supervise.
- They should be punctual and carry their resource file with them.
- Teachers should issue credit slips for positive behaviour.
- For minor breaches of the school rules, some of the following strategies may be used:
  - Call the student aside and motivate him or her towards acceptable behaviour.
  - Sit the student out of the play area for a few minutes.
  - Have the student walk with the teacher.
- Demerit slips should be issued for more serious offences or repetitive misbehaviour.
- A harassment notice should be issued where appropriate.
- Teachers should use resource files to remind students of school rules, out of bounds areas etc.

Roles and responsibilities of staff

It is expected that the staff of this school will do the following:

- Work at creating a positive school environment and building positive relationships.
- Be familiar with the behaviour management plan (BMP) and its procedures.
- Display school codes and class rules prominently in classrooms.
- Follow the guidelines of the BMP to ensure consistency in the implementation of behaviour management procedures.
- Focus on the behaviour rather than the student.
- In the event of a teacher–student conflict, adopt a non-confrontational problem solving approach of 'we must work this out'.
- Actively support other staff members who may be having behaviour management problems, including relief teachers.
- Fill out their support teacher timetable and be other teachers' support teacher when possible.
- Challenge any students who are out of uniform, and ask to see a uniform pass.
- Check attendance each lesson by checking rolls and filling out daily absentee sheets when appropriate. If students are all present, a nil return should be sent to front office.
- Check that students bring diaries to class and are using them. Do random checks.
- Be punctual to class and when doing yard duty. Take resource file with them. Be familiar with school rules and procedures pertaining to that area.
- Relief teachers need to be familiar with the BMP and have access to a resource file.
- If you have any concerns regarding the behaviour management plan, contact a member of the BMIS (Behaviour Management in Schools) committee, which should meet at least once per term to review the plan.

Roles and responsibilities of care group (home room) teachers

- It is the role of the home room teacher to provide pastoral care to members of his or her home room class. This includes keeping records of student behaviour (both positive and negative), implementing consequences, and directing students through the various intervention procedures where appropriate. They are also the first line of communication to parents regarding student behaviour and progress.

- All home room teachers should have: behaviour management plan, resource file, daily information file, home room file, home room records file and a section of a filing cabinet or an archives box to store student records.

- Home room teachers should collect daily information file (DIF–Blue File) each day from outside staffroom.

- During home room they should go through the following procedures:

1 Notices

- Read notices from 'Daily news bulletin' (DNB).
- Hand out any other notices or letters which may be in DIF; e.g. Fridays – weekly newsletter.

2 Attendance

- Check and record attendance on 'Attendance, uniform and diary records' sheet.
- Write absentees on 'Student absentee slip'. Send to the front office at the end of home room period.
- Collect and record any notes for previous absences. Attach notes to 'Daily absentee report' and send to front office.
- Put 'Absentee note needed' sticker in student diaries for any student who keeps forgetting to bring a note.

3 Uniform

- Check and record incorrect uniform.
- Get student into correct uniform if possible; i.e. remove offending item of clothing, or get a spare uniform from deputy.
- If student is out of uniform issue a 'Uniform pass'.
- If student does not have a note from home, give him or her a level one demerit (for repeat offenders).

4 Diaries

- On Mondays, check and record whether diary has been signed by parents. Sign each diary if it has parent's signature.
- If diary is not signed or student doesn't have it by Tuesday, issue a level one demerit (for repeat offenders)
- Keep checking diaries of those students who have not had their diary signed for the week. Issue level one demerits until they do.
- Write any messages to parents as needed.

5 Credit slips

- Credit slips for your students will be placed in your pigeonhole.
- Record credit slips on 'Credit records' sheet.
- Issue students with 'Credit slip given' diary sticker or stamp.
- Put credit slip in lucky draw box.
- On Fridays, draw out prize winners.
- After the draw, file credit slips in the 'Student records' section of the 'Home room file'.
- Issue credit slips for any positive behaviour; e.g. returning absentee note promptly.
- Get 'Credit award certificates' typed up when students accumulate 20 (bronze) or 40 (silver) credit slips. These will be presented at an assembly.

6 Demerit slips

- Demerit slips will be placed in your pigeonhole.
- Record demerits on 'Demerit records' sheet.
- File slips in 'Student records' section of 'Home room file'.
- If a student accumulates 3 level one demerits in one term, issue a community service notice. Issue student with a 'Community service given' diary stamp.
- Intervention point – Students who accumulate three COMMUNITY SERVICES in one term should be referred to the student services team, and parents should be contacted by the home room teacher through either a letter of concern or a phone call.
- Intervention point – If a student gets four or more COMMUNITY SERVICES in one term, a parent interview should be requested by the home room teacher.
- If a student accumulates 3 level two demerits in one term, issue a lunch detention notice. Student needs to bring that back to you for filing, after being signed by detention teacher and parent.
- Write students' names on daily absentee sheet during home room on the day that they are to do detention. Issue student with 'lunch detention given' diary stamp.
- If a student accumulates 3 or more lunch detentions, attach duplicate copies of demerit slips to a deputy referral notice and send to deputy.
- Intervention point – Students who accumulate three LUNCH DETENTIONS in one term, should be referred to the student services team, and parents should be contacted by the home room teacher through either a letter of concern or a phone call.
- Intervention point – If a student gets four or more LUNCH DETENTIONS in one term, a parent interview should be requested by the home room teacher.
- Record any level three demerit slips. Any students who need to be referred, send to deputy.

7 Harassment notices

- If student has been referred to you, counsel him or her (and the victim if necessary) and fill out the 'Action taken' section. File the top copy in the 'Student records' section of the 'home room file', and the bottom copy goes into the 'Harassment records file' at the front office.
- If you get a harassment notice with the 'Action taken' section already filled in, file it in the 'Home room file'.
- Issue student with a 'Harassment notice given' diary stamp.

8 Support teacher referral notice

- File notices.
- Issue 'Withdrawn from class' diary stamp.
- Contact parent if student gets 2 support teacher referral notices in one term.

9 Money file

- If 'Money file' is in your DIF (blue file), collect money and record in file.
- Send money and file to front office with daily absentee form.

10 Demerit records sheet

- After entering results for the week, photocopy and put on the BMIS board in the student services/deputy's office each Friday (if it needs updating). This enables BMIS committee and the student services team to identify students at risk. It also enables teachers to see at a glance what home room students are in.

11 Data collection sheets

- In the last week of term, fill out the data collection sheets; i.e. credit summary sheet, demerit summary sheet, and the community service/detentions/suspension and harassment sheet, and give to the BMIS coordinator for tallying. Please have them in by the last day of term.
- New BMIS strategies will be implemented (if needed) according to the results of these sheets.

ROUTINES AND ROLES

Roles and responsibilities of BMIS coordinators and committee

(BMIS = Behaviour Management in Schools)

- To oversee the collaborative development of the behaviour management plan including its compilation, distribution to staff, and updates.
- To ensure all stakeholders have had the chance to have an input into the behaviour management plan.
- To organise the compilation and distribution of other BMIS resources to staff:
  1. Resource files
  2. Care group (home room) records file
  3. BMIS resource centre
  4. School codes
- To set up and maintain the BMIS student records board and the BMIS noticeboard.

- To convene a BMIS committee meeting once per term or as the need arises.
- To write up the BMIS bulletin after each BMIS committee meeting and distribute to staff.
- To solicit feedback from other staff regarding concerns about the behaviour management plan.
- To make sure parents are told of any updates via newsletter.
- To distribute and collect data collection sheets at the end of each term.
- To compile and distribute the BMIS report at the beginning of each term.
- To lead the review and improvement process.

FUNMAN SAYS:

Johnny says to the teacher, 'You wouldn't punish someone for something they hadn't done would you?'

'Of course not', replies the teacher.

'Oh, that's good, because I haven't done my homework.'

RESOURCES

Resources to support a behaviour management system

In this section:

Proformas ◄

Storage and access of resources ◄

Behaviour management plan resources

(NOTE: These are examples of resources as per sample behaviour management plan, page ##)

There are a number of resources and proformas which are used in the implementation of this behaviour management plan.

Each teacher should have:

- A behaviour management plan
- A resource File – a portable A5 file used to store slips, proformas etc. Also contains an easy reference summary of the BMP, including the school codes

Each home room teacher should also have:

- A daily information file
- A care group (home room) records file
- A student archives facility such as a section of a filing cabinet or an archive box to store student records.
- A credit slip tally chart on display in his or her home room class.

Staff should have access to

- A BMIS records board.
- A BMIS bulletin board.
- BMIS resource centre – a set of pigeonholes to store BMIS proformas and resources.

The students should have:

- A diary for parent–teacher communication and to store credit slips.

Classroom should have:

- The school codes on the wall.

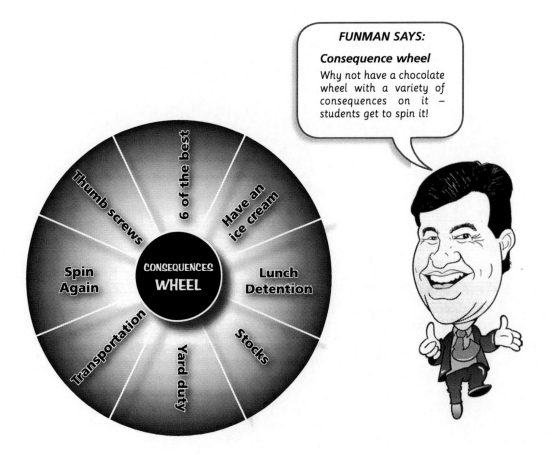

FUNMAN SAYS:

Consequence wheel

Why not have a chocolate wheel with a variety of consequences on it – students get to spin it!

NOTES ABOUT THE FOLLOWING RESOURCES

In order to have uniformity and ease of access, most of these resources are either A5 slips or A4 sheets. The A5 sheets are pre-punched and kept in an A5 resource file which staff can easily carry around. The A4 sheets tend to be more formal letters or forms. These slips and forms are stored in the BMIS resource centre (pigeonholes) for staff to retrieve as they need them.

Credit slips (page 105)

- Credit slips (printed in duplicate) are issued to students for displaying positive behaviour.
- The top copy goes to the student, the bottom copy goes to the home room teacher.
- Each Friday, home room teachers will do a lucky draw with all the credit slips they have received that week.
- If a student receives 20 credit slips in one year, he or she gets a bronze certificate; if 40 a silver certificate.
- If a student gets 60 credit slips in one year, he or she will be presented with a medallion (gold award)

Demerit slips (page 106)

- Demerit slips (printed in duplicate) should be used as a last resort and are issued for continued or serious unacceptable behaviour.
- The actual slip is not given to the student.
- Students are given LEVEL ONE, TWO or THREE demerits, depending on the offence, and they are given either 1, 2 or 3 demerit points in that level, depending on the severity of that offence.
- For LEVEL ONE and TWO offences, both copies go to the home room teacher.
- For LEVEL THREE offences, the top copy goes to the deputy and the bottom copy goes to the home room teacher.
- If a student accumulates 3 lunch detentions (i.e. 9 LEVEL TWO demerits) in one term, the home room teacher sends the deputy a DEPUTY REFERRAL NOTICE, along with the duplicates of the appropriate demerit slips. A DEPUTY REFERRAL NOTICE should be issued for each subsequent lunch detention.

Harassment notices (page 107)

- A harassment notice is issued as a record of any harassment that occurs at school in order to initiate procedures to prevent further conflict.
- The actual slip is not given to the student.
- Once the incident is recorded, the notice should be given to the home room teacher, Year leader, deputy, psychologist or chaplain, depending on the incident.
- Once the 'action taken' section is filled in, the top copy goes to the home room teacher and the bottom copy goes to the harassment records file (front office).

Anecdotal record (page 108)

- **An anecdotal record is issued when:**
  - students are displaying unacceptable behaviour but don't quite warrant a demerit.
  - they are suspected of breaking school rules.
  - they are showing poor attitude or behaviour in a public place such as excursions, sports carnivals, or in front of parents.
  - their behaviour is setting a bad example to younger students.
  - their out of school behaviour is bringing discredit to the school,
  - they are considered 'at risk' for any reason.
- Anecdotal records can be used by home room teachers or deputies to let these students know that their behaviour is unacceptable.
- They can also be used in evidence when students are applying to have their 'good standing' reinstated or are on a 'principal's caution'.

Uniform pass (page 109)

- If a student is out of uniform, the first course of action should be to try and get him or her into correct uniform.
  This can be done by
  (a) removing the offending item of clothing,
  (b) sending him or her to the deputy for a replacement item.
- If a student is out of uniform, he or she should be issued with a uniform pass to carry.
- If he or she doesn't have a note from home regarding being out of uniform, he or she can get a LEVEL ONE demerit.
- If a student is out of uniform and does not have a uniform pass, he or she can be issued with a LEVEL ONE demerit if challenged by a teacher.

Student movement pass (page 110)

- Students out of class or late, with a teacher's permission, should be issued a student movement pass.

Community service (page 111)

- Community service notices are given to students by home room teachers each time they accumulate 3 LEVEL ONE demerits (in one term).
- The type of community service issued is at the discretion of the home room teacher, and may include yard duty, cleaning desks, filing etc.
- Students who accumulate 3 or more community services (in one term) should be referred to the student services team.

Lunch detention notice (page 112)

- The lunch detention notice is given to students by home room teachers each time they accumulate 3 LEVEL TWO demerits (in one term).
- When the student completes the detention, he or she should get the form signed by the detention supervisor and his or her parents before handing back to the home room teacher for filing.
- The 'other/notes' section may be used by the home room teacher to let parents know how the student got the demerits.

Lunch detention self-reflection (page 113)

This sheet is on the reverse of the lunch detention notice and is filled out by students while they are on detention. It aims to help them reflect upon their behaviour and to plan for improvement. It should be signed by the student's parent/guardian before it's returned to the home room teacher.

Class withdrawal notice (page 114)

- Class withdrawal notices (printed in duplicate) are issued to students whom you wish to withdraw from class, either for the remainder of the session, or for a predetermined amount of time.
- All teachers should have completed their support teacher timetable, or a time out room timetable is done.
- Fill out the notice and send the top copy to the support/time out room teacher with the student and give the student a 'Work it out' sheet to do.
- The bottom copy is given to the student's home room teacher for filing. This also lets the home room teacher know he/she should expect a 'Work it out' sheet from the student, signed by his or her parents and the issuing teacher.
- A notice of short-term class withdrawal letter should be sent home to parents.

Class withdrawal 'work it out' sheet (page 115 – 116)

- 'Work it out' sheets should be issued to students when they have been withdrawn from class either as a support teacher referral or time out.
- They are usually issued in conjunction with a class withdrawal notice.
- Once completed, they should be signed by the student, the class teacher and the parent.
- The signed sheet is then given to the student's home room teacher for filing.

CREDIT SLIP

Student's name: _____ Class: _____

Issuing teacher: _____ Date: _____ Term: _____

Home teacher: _____ Recorded: ☐

I appreciate your:

☐ responsible behaviour
☐ caring attitude
☐ improved attitude
☐ improved effort
☐ consistent class effort
☐ excellent class effort
☐ positive contribution
☐ willingness to help
☐ high standards in
☐ class work
☐ assignments
☐ tests

significant improvement in
☐ class work
☐ assignments
☐ tests

☐ correct uniform
☐ school
☐ phys ed

☐ returning note promptly
☐ other _____

Teacher's initials

Top copy to student.
Bottom copy to home room teacher.

CREDIT SLIP

Student's name: _____ Class: _____

Issuing teacher: _____ Date: _____ Term: _____

Home teacher: _____ Recorded: ☐

I appreciate your:

☐ responsible behaviour
☐ caring attitude
☐ improved attitude
☐ improved effort
☐ consistent class effort
☐ excellent class effort
☐ positive contribution
☐ willingness to help
☐ high standards in
☐ class work
☐ assignments
☐ tests

significant improvement in
☐ class work
☐ assignments
☐ tests

☐ correct uniform
☐ school
☐ phys ed

☐ returning note promptly
☐ other _____

Teacher's initials

Top copy to student.
Bottom copy to home room teacher.

R.I.C. Publications   www.ricgroup.com.au   *Behaviour management toolkit*   107

DEMERIT SLIP

Student's name: _____

Issuing teacher: _____   Date: _____

Home teacher: _____   Class: _____   Term: _____   Recorded: ☐

LEVEL 1

NOT TAKING IRRESPONSIBILITY

Needs to learn responsible behaviour.

3 x level 1 demerits = 15 minutes community service

DEMERIT

☐ late to class ①

☐ no diary/not signed

☐ no phys ed uniform ②

☐ incorrect school uniform

☐ not having correct equipment ③

☐ homework/assignment not completed

☐ food past yellow line

☐ other _____

LEVEL 2

NOT BEHAVING RESPONSIBLY

Disturbing the progress of learning.

Needs to make up for lost learning time.

3 x level 2 demerits = Lunch detention

DEMERIT

☐ disturbing other students ①

☐ interrupting teacher ②

☐ failing to follow teacher instructions ③

☐ not completing class work

☐ rough play

☐ swearing

☐ other _____

LEVEL 3

SERIOUS OFFENCES

Inappropriate attitude towards teachers/students.

[Send to deputy]

☐ disobeying teacher   ◯ Sent straight to deputy

☐ insolent behaviour   ◯ Needs to be referred by home room teacher

☐ significant disruption of lesson

☐ other _____

COMMENTS: _____

☐ Teacher's initials

Both copies: To home room teacher
Bottom copy: Sent to deputy by home room teacher when applicable.
Student sent straight to deputy: Top copy – deputy, Bottom copy – home room teacher

Behaviour management toolkit   www.ricgroup.com.au   R.I.C. Publications

DEMERIT SLIP

Student's name: _____

Issuing teacher: _____   Date: _____

Home teacher: _____   Class: _____   Term: _____   Recorded: ☐

LEVEL 1

NOT TAKING IRRESPONSIBILITY

Needs to learn responsible behaviour.

3 x level 1 demerits = 15 minutes community service

DEMERIT

☐ late to class ①

☐ no diary/not signed

☐ no phys ed uniform ②

☐ incorrect school uniform

☐ not having correct equipment ③

☐ homework/assignment not completed

☐ food past yellow line

☐ other _____

LEVEL 2

NOT BEHAVING RESPONSIBLY

Disturbing the progress of learning.

Needs to make up for lost learning time.

3 x level 2 demerits = Lunch detention

DEMERIT

☐ disturbing other students ①

☐ interrupting teacher ②

☐ failing to follow teacher instructions ③

☐ not completing class work

☐ rough play

☐ swearing

☐ other _____

LEVEL 3

SERIOUS OFFENCES

Inappropriate attitude towards teachers/students.

[Send to deputy]

☐ disobeying teacher   ◯ Sent straight to deputy

☐ insolent behaviour   ◯ Needs to be referred by home room teacher

☐ significant disruption of lesson

☐ other _____

COMMENTS: _____

☐ Teacher's initials

Both copies: To home room teacher
Bottom copy: Sent to deputy by home room teacher when applicable.
Student sent straight to deputy: Top copy – deputy, Bottom copy – home room teacher

Behaviour management toolkit   www.ricgroup.com.au   R.I.C. Publications

108

HARASSMENT NOTICE

Student's name: _____ Class: _____

Issuing teacher: _____ Date: _____ Term: _____

Home teacher: _____ Recorded: ☐

This student has been referred to

☐ Home teacher ☐ Deputy ☐ Year leader ☐ Psychologist

for harassing other students.

DETAILS OF INCIDENT

Student(s) harassed: _____

Where did it happen? _____

When did it happen?

☐ Before school ☐ In class ☐ Between class
☐ Recess ☐ Lunch ☐ After school

What happened?

☐ teasing/name calling ☐ physical injury
☐ verbal threats ☐ spreading rumours
☐ threatening with objects ☐ threatening other people
☐ nasty looks/signs/gestures ☐ spitting
☐ property taken or damaged ☐ writing insults (graffiti, notes etc.)
☐ following ☐ other _____

Witness(es): _____

Other details: _____
_____

Action taken: _____
_____
_____

After all details have been completed:
Top copy – home room teacher   Bottom copy – Harassment records file (front office)

HARASSMENT NOTICE

Student's name: _____ Class: _____

Issuing teacher: _____ Date: _____ Term: _____

Home teacher: _____ Recorded: ☐

This student has been referred to

☐ Home teacher ☐ Deputy ☐ Year leader ☐ Psychologist

for harassing other students.

DETAILS OF INCIDENT

Student(s) harassed: _____

Where did it happen? _____

When did it happen?

☐ Before school ☐ In class ☐ Between class
☐ Recess ☐ Lunch ☐ After school

What happened?

☐ teasing/name calling ☐ physical injury
☐ verbal threats ☐ spreading rumours
☐ threatening with objects ☐ threatening other people
☐ nasty looks/signs/gestures ☐ spitting
☐ property taken or damaged ☐ writing insults (graffiti, notes etc.)
☐ following ☐ other _____

Witness(es): _____

Other details: _____
_____

Action taken: _____
_____
_____

After all details have been completed:
Top copy – home room teacher   Bottom copy – Harassment records file (front office)

R.I.C. Publications   www.ricgroup.com.au   *Behaviour management toolkit*   109

ANECDOTAL RECORD

Student's name: _____ Class: _____

Issuing teacher: _____ Date: _____ Term: _____

Home teacher: _____ Recorded: ☐

The above student is causing concern because of:

☐ poor attitude
☐ poor behaviour
☐ lack of courtesy and respect towards others
☐ suspected smoking or other drug use at school
☐ suspected selling of drugs at school
☐ suspected sexual abuse
☐ a risk of self-harm
☐ reports of antisocial behaviour outside of school
☐ actions bringing discredit to the school
☐ other _____

Details: _____
_____
_____
_____
_____

Persons notified

☐ Principal ☐ Year leader
☐ Deputy ☐ Home room teacher
☐ Student services ☐ School psychologist
☐ other _____

This record should be filed by home room teachers in the student records section of their care group (home room) records file.

Behaviour management toolkit   www.ricgroup.com.au   R.I.C. Publications

110

ANECDOTAL RECORD

Student's name: _____ Class: _____

Issuing teacher: _____ Date: _____ Term: _____

Home teacher: _____ Recorded: ☐

The above student is causing concern because of:

☐ poor attitude
☐ poor behaviour
☐ lack of courtesy and respect towards others
☐ suspected smoking or other drug use at school
☐ suspected selling of drugs at school
☐ suspected sexual abuse
☐ a risk of self-harm
☐ reports of antisocial behaviour outside of school
☐ actions bringing discredit to the school
☐ other _____

Details: _____
_____
_____
_____
_____

Persons notified

☐ Principal ☐ Year leader
☐ Deputy ☐ Home room teacher
☐ Student services ☐ School psychologist
☐ other _____

This record should be filed by home room teachers in the student records section of their care group (home room) records file.

Behaviour management toolkit   www.ricgroup.com.au   R.I.C. Publications

110

UNIFORM PASS

Student's name: _____ Class: _____

Home room teacher: _____ Date: _____

This student has consulted with me and has permission to be out of uniform for the following items of clothing.

☐ shirt   ☐ skirt
☐ shorts   ☐ top/jumper
☐ pants   ☐ jacket

Note brought from home:

☐ yes   ☐ no

Proper school uniform should be borrowed from deputy's office where possible.

Referred to deputy:

☐ yes   ☐ no

Deputy's signature (when applicable): _____

Students out of uniform and without a uniform pass can expect a LEVEL ONE demerit.

VALID FOR:

UNIFORM PASS

Student's name: _____ Class: _____

Home room teacher: _____ Date: _____

This student has consulted with me and has permission to be out of uniform for the following items of clothing.

☐ shirt   ☐ skirt
☐ shorts   ☐ top/jumper
☐ pants   ☐ jacket

Note brought from home:

☐ yes   ☐ no

Proper school uniform should be borrowed from deputy's office where possible.

Referred to deputy:

☐ yes   ☐ no

Deputy's signature (when applicable): _____

Students out of uniform and without a uniform pass can expect a LEVEL ONE demerit.

VALID FOR:

STUDENT MOVEMENT PASS

Name(s): _____

Issuing teacher: _____ Date: _____ Term: _____

Please excuse the above student(s) for being late/out of class because:

Staff member:
☐ They have been with me.
Signature: _____

Appointment: They have an appointment with:
☐ Principal   ☐ D/Principal   ☐ Psychologist
☐ Other _____
Time of appointment: _____ Signature: _____

Library: They wish to use the library for a period of _____ minutes.
☐ YES: The above student(s) may use the library.
Signature: _____ (Librarian)

Computer room:
They wish to use the computer room for a period of _____ minutes.
☐ YES: The above student/s may use the computer room.
Signature: _____ (Computer teacher)

Sick bay:
☐ They wish to use the sick bay.   Signature: _____

Other: ☐
_____
_____
_____

STUDENT MOVEMENT PASS

Name(s): _____

Issuing teacher: _____ Date: _____ Term: _____

Please excuse the above student(s) for being late/out of class because:

Staff member:
☐ They have been with me.
Signature: _____

Appointment: They have an appointment with:
☐ Principal   ☐ D/Principal   ☐ Psychologist
☐ Other _____
Time of appointment: _____ Signature: _____

Library: They wish to use the library for a period of _____ minutes.
☐ YES: The above student(s) may use the library.
Signature: _____ (Librarian)

Computer room:
They wish to use the computer room for a period of _____ minutes.
☐ YES: The above student/s may use the computer room.
Signature: _____ (Computer teacher)

Sick bay:
☐ They wish to use the sick bay.   Signature: _____

Other: ☐
_____
_____
_____

COMMUNITY SERVICE

Student's name: _____ Class: _____

Issuing teacher: _____ Date: _____ Time: _____

This student has been given community service because:

☐ he or she has accumulated 3 LEVEL ONE demerits

☐ Other/Notes: _____

_____

_____

_____

_____

DAY:	☐ Mon	☐ Tues	☐ Wed	☐ Thurs	☐ Fri
TIME:	☐ recess	☐ lunch	☐ other		
DURATION:	☐ 15 mins	☐ other			
AREA:	☐ canteen	☐ oval	☐ B block		
	☐ primary	☐ other			

COMMUNITY SERVICE COMPLETED

Signature: _____ Duty teacher

Signature: _____ Parent/Guardian

This notice is to be given to your form teacher once it has been signed by the duty teacher and your parent/guardian.

COMMUNITY SERVICE

Student's name: _____ Class: _____

Issuing teacher: _____ Date: _____ Time: _____

This student has been given community service because:

☐ he or she has accumulated 3 LEVEL ONE demerits

☐ Other/Notes: _____

_____

_____

_____

_____

DAY:	☐ Mon	☐ Tues	☐ Wed	☐ Thurs	☐ Fri
TIME:	☐ recess	☐ lunch	☐ other		
DURATION:	☐ 15 mins	☐ other			
AREA:	☐ canteen	☐ oval	☐ B block		
	☐ primary	☐ other			

COMMUNITY SERVICE COMPLETED

Signature: _____ Duty teacher

Signature: _____ Parent/Guardian

This notice is to be given to your form teacher once it has been signed by the duty teacher and your parent/guardian.

R.I.C. Publications   www.ricgroup.com.au   *Behaviour management toolkit*   113

LUNCH DETENTION NOTICE

Student's name: _____ Class: _____

Issuing teacher: _____ Date: _____ Term: _____

Students: Please fill out the self-reflection sheet on the back of this sheet.

This student has been given community service because:

☐ he or she has accumulated 3 LEVEL TWO demerits

☐ Other/Notes: _____

_____

_____

_____

_____

_____

DAY:	☐ Mon	☐ Tues	☐ Wed	☐ Thurs	☐ Fri
TIME:	☐ 1.00–1.30 pm	☐ other			
DURATION:	☐ 30 mins	☐ other			
AREA:	☐ Room 10	☐ Deputy's office			

DETENTION COMPLETED

Signature: _____ Detention supervisor

Signature: _____ Parent/Guardian

This notice is to be given to your home room teacher once it has been signed by the detention supervisor and your parent/guardian.

114 *Behaviour management toolkit* www.ricgroup.com.au R.I.C. Publications

---

LUNCH DETENTION NOTICE

Student's name: _____ Class: _____

Issuing teacher: _____ Date: _____ Term: _____

Students: Please fill out the self-reflection sheet on the back of this sheet.

This student has been given community service because:

☐ he or she has accumulated 3 LEVEL TWO demerits

☐ Other/Notes: _____

_____

_____

_____

_____

_____

DAY:	☐ Mon	☐ Tues	☐ Wed	☐ Thurs	☐ Fri
TIME:	☐ 1.00–1.30 pm	☐ other			
DURATION:	☐ 30 mins	☐ other			
AREA:	☐ Room 10	☐ Deputy's office			

DETENTION COMPLETED

Signature: _____ Detention supervisor

Signature: _____ Parent/Guardian

This notice is to be given to your home room teacher once it has been signed by the detention supervisor and your parent/guardian.

114 *Behaviour management toolkit* www.ricgroup.com.au R.I.C. Publications

LUNCH DETENTION SELF-REFLECTION

Student's name: _____ Class: _____

1. What am I doing wrong to get lunch detentions?

_____
_____

2. Why am I doing these things?

_____
_____

3. What will happen if I continue to get lunch detentions?

_____
_____

4. What can I do to improve my conduct?

_____
_____

DETENTION COMPLETED

Signature: _____ Detention supervisor

Signature: _____ Parent/Guardian

This notice is to be given to your home room teacher once it has been signed by the detention supervisor and your parent/guardian.

LUNCH DETENTION SELF-REFLECTION

Student's name: _____ Class: _____

1. What am I doing wrong to get lunch detentions?

_____
_____

2. Why am I doing these things?

_____
_____

3. What will happen if I continue to get lunch detentions?

_____
_____

4. What can I do to improve my conduct?

_____
_____

DETENTION COMPLETED

Signature: _____ Detention supervisor

Signature: _____ Parent/Guardian

This notice is to be given to your home room teacher once it has been signed by the detention supervisor and your parent/guardian.

R.I.C. Publications   www.ricgroup.com.au   *Behaviour management toolkit*   115

CLASS WITHDRAWAL NOTICE

Go directly to the support teacher or time out room.
Failure to do so will result in suspension from school.

Student's name: _____ Class: _____

Issuing teacher: _____ Date: _____ Term: _____

Home teacher: _____ Recorded: ☐

☐ Support teacher: _____ Room: _____

☐ Time out room

Could you please supervise the above student for the following time: _____

During this time, the student should fill out the *WORK IT OUT* sheet attached.

At the end of this time, please

☐ direct student back to me in the last five minutes with their *WORK IT OUT* sheet.

☐ direct student to report to me in _____ (room) at _____ (time).

☐ release student at the end of the session.

Top copy: Support/Time out teacher   Bottom copy: Home room teacher

---

CLASS WITHDRAWAL NOTICE

Go directly to the support teacher or time out room.
Failure to do so will result in suspension from school.

Student's name: _____ Class: _____

Issuing teacher: _____ Date: _____ Term: _____

Home teacher: _____ Recorded: ☐

☐ Support teacher: _____ Room: _____

☐ Time out room

Could you please supervise the above student for the following time: _____

During this time, the student should fill out the *WORK IT OUT* sheet attached.

At the end of this time, please

☐ direct student back to me in the last five minutes with their *WORK IT OUT* sheet.

☐ direct student to report to me in _____ (room) at _____ (time).

☐ release student at the end of the session

Top copy: Support/Time out teacher   Bottom copy: Home room teacher

116 *Behaviour management toolkit*   www.ricgroup.com.au   R.I.C. Publications

CLASS WITHDRAWAL *WORK IT OUT* SHEET

VERSION 1

You need to have this signed by the teacher who issued the class withdrawal before you can return to that class.

Student's name: _____ Class: _____

Issuing teacher: _____ Date: _____ Term: _____

Home teacher: _____ Recorded:

What did you do to get withdrawn from class?

_____

_____

How does your behaviour affect the teacher and the rest of the class?

_____

_____

What can you do in the future to prevent this behaviour from happening again?

_____

_____

Signature: _____ (Student)

I am willing to have this student return to my class.

Signature: _____ (Teacher)

Signature: _____ (Parent/Guardian)

This sheet should be given to your home room teacher when signed by your parent/guardian and the issuing teacher.

CLASS WITHDRAWAL *WORK IT OUT* SHEET

VERSION 1

You need to have this signed by the teacher who issued the class withdrawal before you can return to that class.

Student's name: _____ Class: _____

Issuing teacher: _____ Date: _____ Term: _____

Home teacher: _____ Recorded:

What did you do to get withdrawn from class?

_____

_____

How does your behaviour affect the teacher and the rest of the class?

_____

_____

What can you do in the future to prevent this behaviour from happening again?

_____

_____

Signature: _____ (Student)

I am willing to have this student return to my class.

Signature: _____ (Teacher)

Signature: _____ (Parent/Guardian)

This sheet should be given to your home room teacher when signed by your parent/guardian and the issuing teacher.

R.I.C. Publications   www.ricgroup.com.au   *Behaviour management toolkit*   117

WORK IT OUT SHEET

VERSION 2

Name: _____ **Class:** _____ **Date:** _____

Answer the questions on this form neatly and carefully and then hand it back to the teacher from whose class you were withdrawn. He/She must be satisfied with your answers before you return to their class.

1. Why have you been withdrawn from class?

    _____

    _____

2. Have you been told about this behaviour before? _____

    If YES, when? _____

3. Does this behaviour occur in different subjects? _____

4. What are the consequences of missing class time?

    _____

    _____

5. If you were a teacher, how would you have dealt with this?

    _____

    _____

6. How can you *WORK IT OUT* with your teacher?

    _____

    _____

7. What can you do to make sure you don't get withdrawn again?

    _____

    _____

8. Would you like to talk to another teacher or someone from the student services team about how you can WORK IT OUT with your teacher?

    _____

Signed: _____ **(student)** **Date:** _____

I am willing to have return _____ to my class.

Signed: _____ (Student) Date: _____

Signed: _____ (Parent/Guardian) Date: _____

SUPPORT TEACHER / TIME OUT TIMETABLE EXAMPLE

The following teachers are available to take students who have been withdrawn from class. Please check with them first before sending students if possible. Students should have a CLASS WITHDRAWAL NOTICE and a WORK IT OUT sheet.

SESSION	MONDAY	TUESDAY	WEDNESDAY	THURSDAY	FRIDAY
1	Samuels Room 5	Matthews Room 18	Jones Room 7	Taylor Room 1	Wallace Art Room
2	Properjohn Room 5	Lewis Room 12	Pretsel Room 13	Molinari Room 2	Koutsoukis Library
RECESS					
3	Lawrence Room 8	Bartrop Room 8	Harwood Room 2	Geary Room 6	McDonald Room 5
4	Fleay Room 18	Clarke Room 16	Murray Room 3	Hanstrom Room 14	Bryant Room 5
LUNCH	Detention Room	Detention Room	Detention Room	Detention Room	Detention Room
5	Bailey Room 3	Pervan Room 17	Rogers Room 12	Tomka Room 8	Hertzig Room 5

Ideally, there should be the option of sending students to a number of different rooms. In larger schools, staff may supervise a time out room if feasible.

BEHAVIOUR MANAGEMENT PROGRAM
Notice of class withdrawal

Date _____

Dear _____

This is to inform you that your son/daughter _____ was withdrawn from his/her normal class and placed in the care of another teacher.

This is a consequence as outlined in our school behaviour management plan and was due to continued inappropriate behaviour in his/her class.

In an attempt to prevent this behaviour from re-occurring, your son/daughter has been asked to fill out a *WORK IT OUT* sheet. Could you please sign it and return it to the school?

We appreciate your support, so please phone the school or make an appointment if you would like to discuss the matter further.

Yours sincerely

_____

Teacher or Deputy

- -

Dear _____

This is to acknowledge receipt of the letter regarding _____'s inappropriate behaviour at school.

❏   I would like to make an appointment

❏   I don't wish to make an appointment at this stage

Signed _____   Date _____

BEHAVIOUR MANAGEMENT PROGRAM
Notice of extended class withdrawal

Date _____

Dear _____

This is to inform you that your son/daughter _____ has been withdrawn from _____ for a period of _____ and will be placed in the care of other teachers.

This is a consequence as outlined in our school behaviour management plan and was due to continued inappropriate behaviour.

Your child will still continue his/her educational program with set work from his/her teacher(s).

We are very keen to help your child improve his/her behaviour. Could you please phone the school to make an appointment so we can discuss ways of assisting him/her?

Yours sincerely

_____

Teacher or Deputy

Dear _____

This is to acknowledge receipt of the letter regarding _____'s withdrawal from class.

Signed _____   Date _____

BEHAVIOUR MANAGEMENT PROGRAM
In school suspension notice

Date _____

Dear _____

This is to inform you that your son/daughter _____ will be withdrawn from normal classes and will be placed on in-school suspension for the following unacceptable behaviour:

_____

_____

_____

_____

The period of in-school suspension is from _____ until _____ . This is a consequence as outlined in our school behaviour management plan. He/She will continue with his/her educational program separated from other students. He/She will have a different lunchtime and recess break.

We are very keen to help your child to improve his/her behaviour and appreciate your support, so please phone the school or make an appointment if you would like to discuss the matter further.

Yours sincerely

_____

Teacher or Deputy

- -

Dear _____

This is to acknowledge receipt of the letter regarding _____'s in school suspension.

Signed _____   Date _____

BEHAVIOUR MANAGEMENT PROGRAM
Out-of-school suspension notice

Date _____

Dear _____

This is to inform you that your son/daughter _____ has been suspended from school for the following unacceptable behaviour:

_____

_____

_____

_____

Suspension category _____

Number of days _____

Suspension period _____

Date student due back at school _____

Number of days suspended this year _____

This is a consequence as outlined in our school behaviour management plan. The student will be given work to do by his/her teachers so he/she can continue his/her educational program at home.

We are very keen to help your child to improve his/her behaviour and appreciate your support. Please make an appointment so we can discuss strategies to help your child reach his/her educational potential.

Yours sincerely

_____
Deputy

Copy to: ❏ Parent/Guardian ❏ Home room teacher
❏ File ❏ District education authority

Deputy referral notice (page 126)

- These are for use by <u>home room teachers only</u> when students have accumulated three or more lunch detentions.
- Home room teachers attach copies of the demerit slips that have led to the lunch detentions and give to deputy.
- This enables deputies to see what students have being doing wrong. Deputies then issue the appropriate consequence.

Consequence notice (page 127)

- These are issued by deputy only.
- They are given to home room teachers for filing and recording.
- They let home room teachers know about serious offences and what consequences have been given.

Application to reinstate good standing (page 128)

- All students start off the term in 'good standing'.
- Students who incur a lunch or after school detention, a short-term or extended class withdrawal, an in-school or out-of-school suspension, or any serious consequences, lose their 'good standing' and will not be automatically invited to the end of term reward or socials.
- Students may apply to their home room teacher to have their good standing reinstated. The home room teacher may approve this if they have shown a pattern of improved behaviour.
- The application must also be approved by the deputy or Year leader.
- The application process should culminate in the students visiting the deputy or Year leader with their application for final approval.

Demerit lines (page 129)

Demerit lines can be issued with a demerit slip or can be used as an alternative consequence.

Student apology note (page 130)

- This note is written by the student to apologise for inappropriate behaviour.
- It may be written to another student, a teacher, a parent or a community member.
- The person who receives the note may keep it or pass it on to the student's home room teacher for filing if appropriate.

Chill out pass (page 131)

- A 'chill out' pass can be issued to students instead of just 'sending them out of the room'.
- Students should be isolated but in view of the teacher.
- A 'chill out' pass can also be issued instead of giving a demerit and serve as a warning of inappropriate behaviour.

DEPUTY REFERRAL NOTICE

HOME ROOM TEACHER USE ONLY

For use as a cover sheet for demerit slip duplicates when students have accumulated three or more lunch detentions.

Use a demerit slip if you need to refer a student for a specific incident.

Student's name: _____ Class: _____

Issuing teacher: _____ Date: _____

Home teacher: _____ Term: _____

This student has been referred to you because:

he/she has accumulated [ ] lunch detentions.

HOME ROOM TEACHERS PLEASE ATTACH COPIES OF DEMERIT SLIPS

DEPUTY REFERRAL NOTICE

HOME ROOM TEACHER USE ONLY

For use as a cover sheet for demerit slip duplicates when students have accumulated three or more lunch detentions.

Use a demerit slip if you need to refer a student for a specific incident.

Student's name: _____ Class: _____

Issuing teacher: _____ Date: _____

Home teacher: _____ Term: _____

This student has been referred to you because:

he/she has accumulated [ ] lunch detentions.

HOME ROOM TEACHERS PLEASE ATTACH COPIES OF DEMERIT SLIPS

DEPUTY USE ONLY

CONSEQUENCE NOTICE

Student's name: _____ Class: _____

Deputy concerned: _____ Date: _____ Term: _____

Home room teacher: _____ Recorded: ☐

TO THE HOME ROOM TEACHER

The above student has been given:

☐ lunch detention

☐ after school detention

☐ short-term class withdrawal

☐ extended class withdrawal

☐ in-school suspension

☐ out-of-school suspension

☐ other _____

Because: ☐ he/she has accumulated ☐ _____ lunch detentions

☐ other _____

Details: _____

_____

Number of days given ☐

Date/s consequence to be done: _____

DEPUTY USE ONLY

CONSEQUENCE NOTICE

Student's name: _____ Class: _____

Deputy concerned: _____ Date: _____ Term: _____

Home room teacher: _____ Recorded: ☐

TO THE HOME ROOM TEACHER

The above student has been given:

☐ lunch detention

☐ after school detention

☐ short-term class withdrawal

☐ extended class withdrawal

☐ in-school suspension

☐ out-of-school suspension

☐ other _____

Because: ☐ he/she has accumulated ☐ _____ lunch detentions

☐ other _____

Details: _____

_____

Number of days given ☐

Date/s consequence to be done: _____

APPLICATION TO REINSTATE GOOD STANDING

- Application should be made at least one week before the event concerned.
- This completed application should be handed to your home room teacher for consideration
- It must also be approved by the relevant deputy or Year leader.

Student's name: _____ Class: _____

Event(s) concerned: _____

Home room teacher: _____ Date of event: _____

Why do you feel that your *Good Standing* should be reinstated?

_____
_____
_____

Signed: _____ Date: _____

Your application to reinstate your *Good Standing* has:

☐ **Been approved** ☐ **Not been approved because:**

☐ You have had 3 or more consequences this term.
☐ You have accumulated too many demerits or anecdotal records this term.
☐ An incident of negative behaviour was too recent.
☐ An incident of negative behaviour was too serious.
☐ You have a pattern of inappropriate or uncooperative behaviour.
☐ You have committed a smoking or other drug offence.
☐ Other _____

Signed: Year leader: _____ Date: _____

Deputy: _____ Date: _____

APPLICATION TO REINSTATE GOOD STANDING

- Application should be made at least one week before the event concerned.
- This completed application should be handed to your home room teacher for consideration
- It must also be approved by the relevant deputy or Year leader.

Student's name: _____ Class: _____

Event(s) concerned: _____

Home room teacher: _____ Date of event: _____

Why do you feel that your *Good Standing* should be reinstated?

_____
_____
_____

Signed: _____ Date: _____

Your application to reinstate your *Good Standing* has:

☐ **Been approved** ☐ **Not been approved because:**

☐ You have had 3 or more consequences this term.
☐ You have accumulated too many demerits or anecdotal records this term.
☐ An incident of negative behaviour was too recent.
☐ An incident of negative behaviour was too serious.
☐ You have a pattern of inappropriate or uncooperative behaviour.
☐ You have committed a smoking or other drug offence.
☐ Other _____

Signed: Year leader: _____ Date: _____

Deputy: _____ Date: _____

Behaviour management toolkit www.ricgroup.com.au R.I.C. Publications

128

DEMERIT LINES

Name: _____ Class: _____

> Your actions are not appropriate according to our school code of **rights and responsibilities**. Please copy out the following line 10 times to remind you of your responsibilities within our school. Your writing must be NEAT AND LEGIBLE.

☐ I will show courtesy and respect to others.
☐ I will keep our school environment safe, secure and clean.
☐ I will ensure that there is no disruption to our teaching/learning environment.
☐ I will try to develop my educational potential.
☐ I will respect student, staff and school property.
☐ I will ensure that my actions do not discredit the school.

1. _____
2. _____
3. _____
4. _____
5. _____
6. _____
7. _____
8. _____
9. _____
10. _____

DEMERIT LINES

Name: _____ Class: _____

> Your actions are not appropriate according to our school code of **rights and responsibilities**. Please copy out the following line 10 times to remind you of your responsibilities within our school. Your writing must be NEAT AND LEGIBLE.

☐ I will show courtesy and respect to others.
☐ I will keep our school environment safe, secure and clean.
☐ I will ensure that there is no disruption to our teaching/learning environment.
☐ I will try to develop my educational potential.
☐ I will respect student, staff and school property.
☐ I will ensure that my actions do not discredit the school.

1. _____
2. _____
3. _____
4. _____
5. _____
6. _____
7. _____
8. _____
9. _____
10. _____

STUDENT APOLOGY NOTE

Student's name: _____ Class: _____

Issuing teacher: _____ Date: _____

Home teacher: _____ Term: _____

When writing this note, please indicate:

- what your inappropriate behaviour was,
- how it made the other person(s) feel,
- what you are going to do about it.

Dear _____

_____

_____

_____

_____

_____

_____

To make amends for offending you, I will:

_____

_____

_____

_____

_____

Signed: _____ Date: _____

This sheet should be given to the person to whom you are apologising, who may then give it to your home room teacher.

STUDENT APOLOGY NOTE

Student's name: _____ Class: _____

Issuing teacher: _____ Date: _____

Home teacher: _____ Term: _____

When writing this note, please indicate:

- what your inappropriate behaviour was,
- how it made the other person(s) feel,
- what you are going to do about it.

Dear _____

_____

_____

_____

_____

_____

_____

To make amends for offending you, I will:

_____

_____

_____

_____

_____

Signed: _____ Date: _____

This sheet should be given to the person to whom you are apologising, who may then give it to your home room teacher.

All members of the school community have the:

 Right

- to be treated with courtesy and respect
- to work in and enjoy a safe, secure and clean environment
- to teach and learn without disruption
- to achieve their educational potential
- to have their property respected
- to be proud of their achievements

 **Responsibility**

- to show respect and courtesy to others
- to keep their environment safe, secure and clean
- to ensure that there is no disruption to another person's teaching–learning environment
- to develop their potential and to assist others in doing the same
- to respect student, staff and school property
- to ensure that their actions do not discredit the school

For a full colour version of this template to print out and laminate, visit:

www.behaviourmanagement.net

STUDENT ABSENTEE SLIP

Class: _____   Date: _____

Absentees

Lunch detentions

Catch up tutorials

STUDENT ABSENTEE SLIP

Class: _____   Date: _____

Absentees

Lunch detentions

Catch up tutorials

DAILY NEWS BULLETIN (DNB) MESSAGE

DAY: ☐ Mon ☐ Tues ☐ Wed ☐ Thurs ☐ Fri

DATES OF DNB: _____

NOTICE TO: ☐ staff only ☐ students only ☐ staff and students

YEAR GROUP(S) CONCERNED: _____

Message _____

_____

_____

_____

_____

_____

_____

_____

_____

_____

_____

_____

Notice from: _____ Date: _____

DAILY NEWS BULLETIN (DNB) MESSAGE

DAY: ☐ Mon ☐ Tues ☐ Wed ☐ Thurs ☐ Fri

DATES OF DNB: _____

NOTICE TO: ☐ staff only ☐ students only ☐ staff and students

YEAR GROUP(S) CONCERNED: _____

Message _____

_____

_____

_____

_____

_____

_____

_____

_____

_____

_____

_____

Notice from: _____ Date: _____

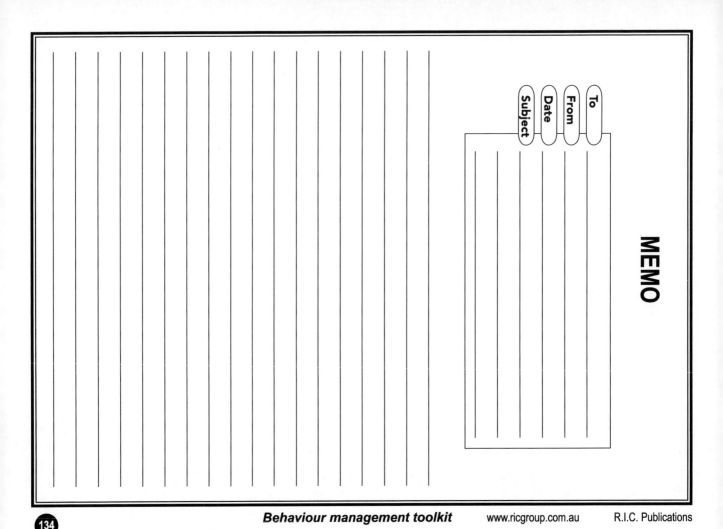

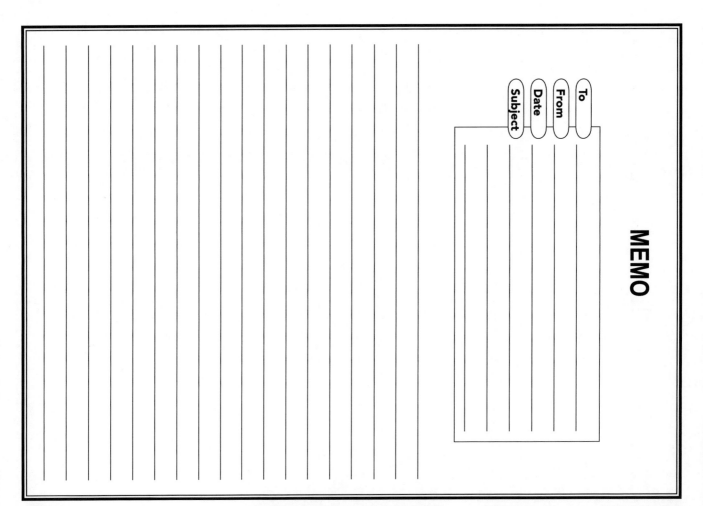

CERTIFICATE OF APPRECIATION

For the positive contributions made to

Our School

(**Bronze**) (**Silver**) (**Gold**)

Award

_____

has received 20/40/60 credit slips.

The staff and students appreciate your efforts.

OUR SCHOOL VISION

*'A school community where individuals seek academic, creative and physical
excellence to achieve their potential with respect and irresponsibility towards
themselves, others and the environment.'*

_____   _____

HOME ROOM TEACHER   PRINCIPAL

                                                                     Date: _____

LETTER OF COMMENDATION

Date _____

Dear _____

Through my role as home room teacher, a large part of the school's pastoral care responsibility for your child falls to me. It is my task to keep tabs on attendance, uniforms, general behaviour, academic progress and use of diaries. I am also your point of contact if you have any concerns regarding your child's progress.

It has come to my attention that _____ has been making a positive contribution to our school community.

We wish to congratulate your son/daughter for the following:

❏ Responsible behaviour   ❏ Willingness to help

❏ Caring attitude   ❏ High standards in class work

❏ Great cooperation   ❏ High standards in tests

❏ Consistent class effort   ❏ High standards in assignments

❏ Excellent class effort   ❏ Improvement in class work

❏ Improved attitude   ❏ Improvement in tests

❏ Improved effort   ❏ Improvement in assignments

❏ Positive contribution   ❏ Excellent diary use

❏ Other _____

The positive contribution your child makes to our school is greatly appreciated by all. Thank you for your continued support of our school.

Yours sincerely

_____

Homeroom teacher

LETTER OF CONCERN

Date _____

Dear _____

Through my role as home room teacher, a large part of the school's pastoral care responsibility for your child falls to me. It is my task to keep tabs on attendance, uniforms, general behaviour, academic progress and use of diaries. I am also your point of contact if you have any concerns regarding your child's progress.

It has come to my attention that _____ has been causing concern in the following area(s):

- ❏ Late to class
- ❏ Diary not signed
- ❏ Incorrect school uniform
- ❏ Not having correct equipment
- ❏ Not completing homework/assignments
- ❏ Not completing class work
- ❏ Difficulty with class work
- ❏ Unsatisfactory behaviour
- ❏ Poor attitude
- ❏ Other _____

With your help, we would like to curb this trend. If you would like to discuss these matters (or any others), please feel free to contact me at the school.

Thank you for your assistance in this matter, and for your continuing support of the school.

Yours sincerely

_____
Homeroom teacher

NOTICE OF UNSATISFACTORY PROGRESS

Student's name: _____   Home room: _____

Class subject: _____   Date: _____

Teacher: _____

Dear Parent/Guardian,

This is to inform you that your son/daughter:

☐ is not making adequate progress in this class/subject.

☐ is likely to fail this subject.

We would like to bring to your attention the following concerns about your child's performance which are affecting his/her progress:

BEHAVIOUR

☐ Disturbs other students   ☐ Insolent/disrespectful
☐ Interrupts the teacher   ☐ Disrupts the lesson
☐ Fails to follow teacher's instructions

ORGANISATION

☐ Doesn't have correct equipment   ☐ Is not using diary
☐ Doesn't catch up on missed work

ATTITUDE/EFFORT

☐ Doesn't settle down to work   ☐ Works too slowly
☐ Gives up too easily   ☐ Careless approach to work
☐ Relies on teacher too heavily instead of using own initiative

LEARNING

☐ Weakness in oral work   ☐ Weakness in written work
☐ Difficulty in understanding key concepts   ☐ Weakness in comprehension
☐ Fails to complete class work   ☐ Poor test results
☐ Fails to complete homework/assignments   ☐ Poor attendance

OTHER

We believe that you should be aware of these concerns and we would like to work with you to take appropriate action in order to improve your child's performance. Should you wish to discuss your child's progress, please contact me at school at your earliest convenience.

Yours sincerely

_____

Teacher

STUDENT PROGRESS REPORT

Date: _____

Student:	Home room:
Number of days absent:	Number of credit awards:

Desired outcomes	Never or rarely	Sometimes	Usually	Always
Demonstrates positive behaviour				
Cooperates with others				
Wears correct school uniform				
Comes prepared for class				
Participates in class activities				
Participates in discussions				
Works well independently				
Completes all class work				
Completes homework/assignments				
Understands lesson content				
Asks for help if needed				

Number of consequences	
Community service	
Lunch detentions	
Short-term class withdrawal	
Extended class withdrawal	
In-school suspension	
Out-of-school suspension	

Comments: _____

_____

_____

_____   _____
HOME ROOM TEACHER   PRINCIPAL

PRINCIPAL'S CAUTION

Date _____

Dear _____

Records held by the school indicate that your general behaviour this year has been unacceptable.

As you are aware, certain privileges are extended to all students. These include camps, the reward afternoon, socials and graduation events. You are also aware that these privileges must be earnt, they are not a right.

This letter serves as a **formal caution** (or warning) to you. Any further reports of unacceptable behaviour by you will be **submitted to me**. It is highly probable that the first such report will mean that you will not be invited to the

_____ .

Yours sincerely

_____
Principal

PARENT CONTACT RECORD

Student's name: _____ Class: _____

Issuing teacher: _____ Date: _____

Home room teacher: _____ Term: _____

CONVERSATION

☐ Phone call
☐ Parent interview
☐ Case conference
☐ Incident meeting
☐ Other _____

CORRESPONDENCE

☐ Letter of commendation
☐ Notice of unsatisfactory progress
☐ Extended class withdrawal notice
☐ School reminders fridge magnet
☐ Other _____
☐ Letter of concern
☐ Class withdrawal notice
☐ Student progress report
☐ Principal's caution

SUBJECT OF CONTACT

☐ Behaviour
☐ Organisation
☐ Attitude/Effort
☐ Learning
☐ Other _____
☐ Class work
☐ Homework
☐ Attendance
☐ General

Details: _____
_____
_____
_____
_____
_____

PARENT CONTACT RECORD

Student's name: _____ Class: _____

Issuing teacher: _____ Date: _____

Home room teacher: _____ Term: _____

CONVERSATION

☐ Phone call
☐ Parent interview
☐ Case conference
☐ Incident meeting
☐ Other _____

CORRESPONDENCE

☐ Letter of commendation
☐ Notice of unsatisfactory progress
☐ Extended class withdrawal notice
☐ School reminders fridge magnet
☐ Other _____
☐ Letter of concern
☐ Class withdrawal notice
☐ Student progress report
☐ Principal's caution

SUBJECT OF CONTACT

☐ Behaviour
☐ Organisation
☐ Attitude/Effort
☐ Learning
☐ Other _____
☐ Class work
☐ Homework
☐ Attendance
☐ General

Details: _____
_____
_____
_____
_____
_____

RESCUE AND SUPPORT

Support services infrastructure – pastoral care for students and staff

In this section:

Support services for students ◄

Intervention and corrective strategies ◄

Support systems for staff ◄

Support systems for students

An integral part of any behaviour management system are mechanisms to help 'rescue' or provide pastoral care for any members of the school community who are experiencing difficulties, including students, parents and staff.

The student services team

A student services team is a group of people whose role is to implement initiatives to help promote a positive, safe and caring school environment, and to assist students (and their parents) who are having problems at school by providing counselling, improvement strategies, life skills courses and/or referrals to other agencies. The team should not be seen as a panacea for teacher's problems, but more as a resource to support teachers in dealing with students who are causing concern.

The team may comprise a number of different personnel, depending on the size of the school and the resources they have allocated to student support services. The roles of these people may be on a full-time or part-time basis, or they may be accessed from local education agencies on a regular or 'as needed' basis.

Some of these roles may include:

- Student services coordinator
- Pastoral care coordinator
- Intervention officer
- Year group coordinator
- School psychologist
- Chaplain
- Nurse
- Police officer
- Community volunteers/mentors

Intervention and corrective strategies

A student services team can offer services such as:

- Identification of students at risk.
- Individual counselling.

- Specialised small-group workshops in:
  - Anger management
  - Study habits and time management
  - Self-esteem
  - Conflict resolution and mediation skills
  - Protective behaviours
  - General social skills
- Assessing for learning difficulties – developing strategies to assist.
- Learning support – setting up individual learning programs.
- Referral to outside agencies and exploring alternative schooling for students experiencing difficulties in the mainstream.
- Behaviour management strategies for individuals or groups of students.
- Mediation between parties in conflict.
- Bullying and teasing workshops – raising awareness and teaching skills to cope.
- Parenting programs or individual counselling on parenting skills.
- Coordination of peer support programs
- Coordination of alcohol-free and drug-free school holiday activities.
- Provide a link for students to community groups.

Support from students

The student services team may train and utilise students in support roles such as:

- Peer support groups
- Peer mediators
- Peer counsellors

DIMENSION 7

Safe havens

Areas (such as a section of the library) where potential victims can go during breaktime. A bit like a safety house.

Students can be referred to the student services team at any time if they are considered 'at risk' (e.g. behaviourally, socially or academically). However, they should be referred at certain intervention points as outlined by the school's behaviour management plan.

Example of intervention points

The behaviour management plan has a series of intervention points.

When a student reaches certain consequences for inappropriate behaviour, various intervention and corrective strategies are implemented to try to change this behaviour.

At these intervention points the following procedures may be used:

- Letters of concern or phone calls to parents.
- Referrals to the student services team for counselling or specialised courses.
- Parent interviews.
- Case conferences.
- Referrals to the police (in the case of incidents involving drugs or other serious offences)

Below is a list of intervention points.

3 COMMUNITY SERVICES

➤ Letter of concern or phone call to parent plus
➤ Student services referral.

4 COMMUNITY SERVICES

➤ Parent interview requested.
➤ 'School reminders' fridge magnet sent home.

3 LUNCH DETENTIONS

➤ Letter of concern or phone call to parent plus
➤ Student services referral.

(in or out of school – in one year)

4 LUNCH DETENTIONS

➤ Parent interview requested.

2 HARASSMENT NOTICES

➤ Parent should be contacted by home room teacher.

CLASS WITHDRAWAL

➤ Parent should be contacted by home room teacher.

LEVEL THREE CONSEQUENCES

➤ Deputy contacts parents if appropriate.

10 DAYS' ACCUMULATED SUSPENSION

Deputy convenes a case conference with student, parent(s), school psychologist, home room teacher, principal or deputy and a representative from the local education authority.

INCIDENTS INVOLVING DRUGS OR OTHER SERIOUS OFFENCES

Deputy may refer student(s) to the police service for counselling or legal consequences.

Although these procedures are put into practice after reaching these intervention points, any student who is considered 'at risk' (e.g. behaviourally, socially or academically) can be referred to the student services team, and/or parents can be contacted at any time.

RESCUE AND SUPPORT

Student services referral notice (page 147)

A student services referral notice is issued if:

- a student is considered 'at risk' for any reason (e.g. behaviourally, socially or academically),
- he/she accumulates 3 community services (in one term).
- he/she accumulates 3 lunch detentions (in one term), the notice should be given to home room teacher once it is completed.

Student's chill out pass (page 149)

- Can be issued by deputies in extreme cases for students known to have a volatile temper.
- Students should hand the pass politely to their class teacher if they feel under pressure and ask to sit outside the deputy's office.
- Deputies will notify staff of students who have been issued one.

School reminders (page 149)

- A 'School reminders' fridge magnet card can be sent home by the home room teacher if appropriate.

- Just laminate the print-outs and stick fridge magnets on the back.

STUDENT SERVICES REFERRAL NOTICE

Student's name: _____ Class: _____

Issuing teacher: _____ Date: _____ Term: _____

Home teacher: _____ Recorded: ☐

This student has been referred to

☐ Year coordinator ☐ Chaplain ☐ School psychologist ☐ Other

Because:

☐ He/She has accumulated ☐ community services

☐ He/She has accumulated ☐ lunch detentions

☐ Other _____

Please tick areas of concern:

☐ Disruptive behaviour ☐ Homework

☐ Harassing others ☐ Learning difficulties

☐ Being harassed ☐ Uniform

☐ Drug use ☐ Lateness
(including smoking, marijuana, alcohol etc.)

☐ Aggressive behaviour ☐ Organisation

☐ Depressive behaviour ☐ Attendance issues

☐ Grief through loss
(including death, separation, moving schools etc.)

Comments: _____
_____

Action taken: _____

Signature (Student services): _____

To be given to home room teacher after all details have been completed.

R.I.C. Publications   www.ricgroup.com.au   *Behaviour management toolkit*   **147**

STUDENT SERVICES REFERRAL NOTICE

Student's name: _____ Class: _____

Issuing teacher: _____ Date: _____ Term: _____

Home teacher: _____ Recorded: ☐

This student has been referred to

☐ Year coordinator ☐ Chaplain ☐ School psychologist ☐ Other

Because:

☐ He/She has accumulated ☐ community services

☐ He/She has accumulated ☐ lunch detentions

☐ Other _____

Please tick areas of concern:

☐ Disruptive behaviour ☐ Homework

☐ Harassing others ☐ Learning difficulties

☐ Being harassed ☐ Uniform

☐ Drug use ☐ Lateness
(including smoking, marijuana, alcohol etc.)

☐ Aggressive behaviour ☐ Organisation

☐ Depressive behaviour ☐ Attendance issues

☐ Grief through loss
(including death, separation, moving schools etc.)

Comments: _____
_____

Action taken: _____

Signature (Student services): _____

To be given to home room teacher after all details have been completed.

R.I.C. Publications   www.ricgroup.com.au   *Behaviour management toolkit*   **147**

Teacher: _____

STUDENTS AT EDUCATIONAL RISK SAFETY NET

Dear staff member,

We would like to identify any students causing concern and those strategies which have been used to assist them. Could you please list any student you consider 'at risk'?

Time period: _____

Name	Behaviour/learning/other	Parent contact					Referrals – Counselling or remediation						Monitoring progress					
	B/L/O	Note in Student Diary	Letter of concern	Phone call	Parent interview	Case conference	Home room teacher	Year coordinator	Chaplain	School psychologist	Remediation	Tutoring	Care group (home room) records	Daily progress report	Daily goal report	Behaviour and progress report	Student contract	Other

For a full-colour version of these templates to print out and laminate, visit:

www.behaviourmanagement.net

Individual education/behaviour plan development process

Gather student information (from school records, teachers, outside agencies)

- Background – history
- School results
- Organisation and work habits
- Screening
- Medical
- Behaviour patterns
- Learning
- Previous intervention

Determine priorities

- Desired outcomes for student

Establish benchmarks to measure improvement

- For example, latest school report

Set long-term goals

Set short-term goals

- Identify specific behaviours that need to be addressed

Select strategies and resources to address these behaviours

Implement the program

- Collaboratively develop the plan (coordinator, student, parents, psychologist)
- Strategies
- Subjects/teachers involved
- Duration
- Communicating to all stakeholders

Monitor student progress

- Regular parent contact – set time
- Daily progress report
- Behaviour and progress report
- Diary entries
- Student interviews – set time
- Daily goal report
- Student contract

Set a time line

Establish review processes

- Who?
- Where?
- When?
- How?

Individual education/behaviour plan development

Examples of possible strategies

Behaviour

- Teachers use positive reinforcement often – credit slips or other.
- Parents to reinforce credit slips with rewards at home.
- Issue a warning/rule reminder before consequence so that the student is making the choice to receive that consequence – normal school rules still apply.
- Use consequences from home; e.g. not allowed to use computer.

Organisation and work habits

- Glue student timetable into student's file/book, have spare copies available.
- Checklist of routines/instructions on student's desk.
- Have spare equipment/materials for student.
- Sit student at the front of the class in a position where teacher can make eye contact (same seat every lesson).
- Sit student away from windows or stimuli which could distract him or her.
- Student to be paired up or be in close proximity to good role models.
- Make student clearly aware of class rules; e.g. a list near him or her.
- Give student tasks which enables him or her to move out of his or her seat occasionally; e.g. clean the board, run an errand.

- Develop consistent class routines.
- Subtle signal to indicate to student to get back on task – not rebuke; e.g. tap desk.
- Lunch – place regular order at canteen – prepay.

Learning

- Write tasks to be completed on the board.
- Provide photocopied notes for student.
- Break complex tasks into smaller units.
- Allow student to hand in assignments in parts.
- Increase time given to complete assignments.
- Give oral tests or assignments.
- Allow student to use a calculator.
- Use a computer if possible.
- Determine student's preferred learning style – set class work and assessment tasks accordingly.

Referrals

- Refer to student services team for specific course.
- Employ a tutor.

Diagnostic testing

Reading ☐
Writing ☐
Numeracy ☐

Assessment for

ADHD ☐
Dyslexia ☐
Other ☐
_____

Referrals to

School chaplain ☐
School psychologist ☐
Speech therapist ☐
Occupational therapy ☐
Dietitian ☐
Clinical psychologist ☐
Social worker ☐
Paediatrician ☐

NB: Students must still obey school rules and follow the instructions of their teachers.

DAILY PROGRESS REPORT

VERSION 1

This student has been placed on a daily progress report. If his or her behaviour is unsatisfactory while on this report, he or she may be given a short-term class withdrawal or other consequences.

It is the student's responsibility to make sure this daily progress report is completed.

Student:	Home room:
Minimum number of days:	Starting date:
Placed on report by:	

Day			Date	
Session	Subject/Class	Comment		Teacher's signature
1				
2				
3				
4				
5				
Signed by parent/guardian			Signed by issuer	

Day			Date	
Session	Subject/Class	Comment		Teacher's signature
1				
2				
3				
4				
5				
Signed by parent/guardian			Signed by issuer	

This sheet should be shown to the issuing teacher/coordinator each morning for signing.

Day			Date	
Session	**Subject/Class**	**Comment**		**Teacher's signature**
1				
2				
3				
4				
5				
Signed by parent/guardian			**Signed by issuer**	

Day			Date	
Session	**Subject/Class**	**Comment**		**Teacher's signature**
1				
2				
3				
4				
5				
Signed by parent/guardian			**Signed by issuer**	

Day			Date	
Session	**Subject/Class**	**Comment**		**Teacher's signature**
1				
2				
3				
4				
5				
Signed by parent/guardian			**Signed by issuer**	

This sheet should be shown to the issuing teacher/coordinator each morning for signing.

DAILY PROGRESS REPORT

VERSION 2

This student has been placed on a daily progress report. If his or her behaviour is unsatisfactory while on this report, he or she may be given a short-term class withdrawal or other consequences.

It is the student's responsibility to make sure this daily progress report is completed.

Student:	Home room:
Minimum number of days:	**Starting date:**
Placed on report by:	

Day			Date	
Session	**Subject/Class**	**Behaviour**	**Class work**	**Teacher's signature/comment**
Home-room		❑ Causing concern ❑ Satisfactory	❑ Causing concern ❑ Satisfactory	
1		❑ Causing concern ❑ Satisfactory	❑ Causing concern ❑ Satisfactory	
2		❑ Causing concern ❑ Satisfactory	❑ Causing concern ❑ Satisfactory	
3		❑ Causing concern ❑ Satisfactory	❑ Causing concern ❑ Satisfactory	
4		❑ Causing concern ❑ Satisfactory	❑ Causing concern ❑ Satisfactory	
USSR		❑ Causing concern ❑ Satisfactory	❑ Causing concern ❑ Satisfactory	
5		❑ Causing concern ❑ Satisfactory	❑ Causing concern ❑ Satisfactory	
Signed by parent/guardian			**Signed by Issuer**	

This sheet should be shown to the issuing teacher/coordinator each morning for signing.

DAILY GOAL REPORT

This sheet is to be kept in the red file and carried to every class. It should be filled in by your teacher(s) at the end of each session with them. It is then to be signed by your parents each night and returned to the deputy/Year coordinator/homeroom teacher for the following morning.

Student:		Home room:
Minimum number of days:	**Starting date:**	
Placed on report by:		
Goal for the day:		

Teachers please tick the box if the student has achieved the nominated goal in your lesson.

Session	Goal achieved	Class teacher's comments/signature
1		
2		
3		
4		
5		

Parent's comments

_____
Signature

Home room teacher's comments

_____
Signature

Student's comments

_____
Signature

BEHAVIOUR AND PROGRESS SHEET

To be filled out by the teachers of the following student.

Student: _____ Home room: _____ Date: _____

Session	Teacher	Behaviour	Class work	Comment
Home room		☐ Causing concern ☐ Satisfactory	☐ Causing concern ☐ Satisfactory	
English		☐ Causing concern ☐ Satisfactory	☐ Causing concern ☐ Satisfactory	
Maths		☐ Causing concern ☐ Satisfactory	☐ Causing concern ☐ Satisfactory	
Science		☐ Causing concern ☐ Satisfactory	☐ Causing concern ☐ Satisfactory	
Society and environment		☐ Causing concern ☐ Satisfactory	☐ Causing concern ☐ Satisfactory	
Computing		☐ Causing concern ☐ Satisfactory	☐ Causing concern ☐ Satisfactory	
LOTE		☐ Causing concern ☐ Satisfactory	☐ Causing concern ☐ Satisfactory	
Health education		☐ Causing concern ☐ Satisfactory	☐ Causing concern ☐ Satisfactory	
Physical education		☐ Causing concern ☐ Satisfactory	☐ Causing concern ☐ Satisfactory	
Sport		☐ Causing concern ☐ Satisfactory	☐ Causing concern ☐ Satisfactory	
Whole-school activity		☐ Causing concern ☐ Satisfactory	☐ Causing concern ☐ Satisfactory	
Elective _____		☐ Causing concern ☐ Satisfactory	☐ Causing concern ☐ Satisfactory	
Elective _____		☐ Causing concern ☐ Satisfactory	☐ Causing concern ☐ Satisfactory	

Behaviour management toolkit   www.ricgroup.com.au   R.I.C. Publications

STUDENT CONTRACT

To enable this student to have a more positive learning experience, the following conditions have been mutually agreed upon. The student and his or her parents have agreed that these conditions are fair and reasonable and that the student is capable of achieving them.

Name

Home room

Starting date

Review date

CONDITIONS

I, (the student), agree to the following conditions:

1. I will raise my hand and ask for help if I need it.
2. I will remain seated unless I have been given permission to move.
3. I will not answer back and argue when given instructions.
4. I will not get distracted by others.
5. I will sit upright in my chair.
6. I will arrive for class on time.

CONSEQUENCES

I understand that if I do not abide by these conditions, I will face one or more of the following consequences:

1. Loss of privilege (use of computers or sport).
2. A demerit slip.
3. Isolation within the class.
4. Withdrawal from class.
5. Sent to deputy principal.

SIGNED

Student _____ Date _____

Parent _____ Date _____

Teacher/Year coordinator _____ Date _____

Copy to: ☐ Student ☐ Parents ☐ Home room teacher ☐ Student's class teachers

R.I.C. Publications   www.ricgroup.com.au   *Behaviour management toolkit*   157

CASE CONFERENCE RECORD

(Notes of this meeting to be completed on the back of this sheet.)

School _____ Date _____

Student _____ Class _____

Parent/guardian _____

Address _____

Phone _____

OTHER PARTICIPANTS

Convenor – Psychologist

Home room teacher

CURRENT SITUATION

LONG TERM GOAL/AGREED OUTCOME

SHORT TERM GOAL/AGREED OUTCOME

ACTION TO BE TAKEN

Strategies	By whom	By when

Review date	

CURRENT SITUATION

The action to be taken has been clearly explained to me and I give my permission for it to take place:

Signed: _____ Date: _____

Copy to: ☐ School ☐ Home room teacher ☐ District education office

Behaviour management toolkit   www.ricgroup.com.au   R.I.C. Publications

Staff support checklist

Just as we need mechanisms to help 'rescue' or support students who may be experiencing difficulties at school, we need to provide a supportive environment for our staff. Below is a checklist regarding support for staff in the context of managing student behaviour. How does your school rate?

Pastoral care for staff (staff welfare)	Strongly Agree	Agree	Disagree	Strongly Disagree
Staff welfare is a priority.				
Staff efforts are recognised and acknowledged.				
Staff are supportive of each other in managing student behaviour.				
Staff in the classroom have strong back-up from administration.				
Staff have mechanisms in place to help build and maintain their morale.				
Staff who are experiencing difficulties regarding the management of student behaviour have support mechanisms available to them.				
Staff are aware of and follow appropriate grievance procedures.				
Staff experience Equal Employment Opportunity and Diversity practices being observed.				
Staff feel they are known and valued members of the school community.				

Communication	Strongly Agree	Agree	Disagree	Strongly Disagree
The behaviour management plan is well documented and well known by all stakeholders.				
Staff have easy access to policies and procedures.				
Staff are kept informed of changes to the behaviour management plan.				
Staff are involved in decision-making processes regarding behaviour management issues.				

Roles and responsibilities	Strongly Agree	Agree	Disagree	Strongly Disagree
The spread of responsibility for managing student behaviour is fair and equitable.				
Staff have clearly defined roles within the behaviour management system.				
Staff actually do what is expected of their role.				
If staff aren't doing their job properly, they are assisted to do so or disciplined.				
Staff are recognised and remunerated (time, money or other) for extra duties or responsibilities.				

Personal and professional development	Strongly Agree	Agree	Disagree	Strongly Disagree
Time is allocated to induct staff in the initial implementation of the behaviour management plan.				
Time is allocated to induct new teachers and relief staff.				
Staff are giving training to improve their behaviour management skills.				
Whole-school professional development days include sessions involving collegial and team-building activities.				
Staff have effective performance management practices in place.				

Support systems for staff

Teachers can often feel isolated when it comes to managing student behaviour. Just talking to other teachers and realising that they are facing similar problems can be very therapeutic. Below are some ideas for supporting staff in the management of student behaviour.

Responsibility for staff welfare

- A staff welfare coordinator (we have student services coordinators, why not staff services?)

Developing a supportive staff culture

- Regular collegial and team-building activities to develop a culture of mutual support.

Structured support programs

- Induction program for new teachers regarding the school behaviour management system.
- A mentor system – link experienced teachers with those having difficulties. Can have structured meetings or incidental conversation.
- Behaviour management coach – a key person with expertise in this area who can help those having difficulties.
- Peer support program where teachers can watch each other in action and give constructive advice.
- Access to counselling for teachers experiencing stress.

Assisting with problem students

- **Buddy system** – teachers agree to take troublesome students from each other's classes if needed.
- **Support teacher withdrawal timetable** – a whole-school approach where teachers volunteer to take problem students at certain times of the week – this is recorded on a timetable for whole-school use.
- **A 'time out room'** – to get troublesome students 'out of the teacher's hair' for a while.

Getting help in times of need

- A 'hot spot' timetable where school leaders can anticipate trouble and either visit those classrooms or be prepared for action.
- An 'admin. alert' card which teachers can send to the school leaders team to request urgent assistance.

Learning and improving

- A resource centre of behaviour management materials; e.g. books, videos, website links, PD opportunities and checklists.
- Regular professional development on managing student behaviour.
- Forums to discuss school behaviour management system issues.
- Forums to share effective behaviour management strategies.

Acknowledgment

- Acknowledgment of staff who initiate programs which enhance a positive school environment.

HOT SPOT TIMETABLE EXAMPLE

The following classes are potential trouble spots. Members of the school leaders team should either visit these classes if possible or be prepared for action.

SESSION	MONDAY	TUESDAY	WEDNESDAY	THURSDAY	FRIDAY
1			Year 5￼ Maths￼ Room 7		
2		Year 9￼ Woodwork￼ Room 12		Year 4￼ Science￼ Room 2	Year 8￼ Study Skills￼ Library
RECESS					
3	Year 6￼ Art￼ Room 8			Year 6￼ Music￼ Room 6	
4		Year 3￼ Drama￼ Room 16	Year 7￼ Music￼ Room 3		Year 10￼ Maths￼ Room 5
LUNCH					
5	Year 7￼ Physical Education￼ Oval	Year 9￼ Science￼ Room 17	Year 10￼ Science￼ Room 12		Year 9￼ English￼ Room 5

Admin. Alert

COULD A MEMBER OF THE ADMIN. TEAM PLEASE COME

IMMEDIATELY

Admin. Alert

COULD A MEMBER OF THE ADMIN. TEAM PLEASE COME

IMMEDIATELY

- The admin. alert card is generally coloured red and laminated.
- Teachers who have an emergency or a particularly disobedient student can send this card down to a member of the admin. team who, will immediately recognise that the situation is urgent.

Being ready and resilient

for the complex task of managing student behaviour

Managing student behaviour is not for the faint-hearted and before we can develop positive relationships with others we need to ensure that 'our own house is in order'. Use this checklist to find out how you might improve your readiness and resiliency.

Be resilient	Strongly Agree	Agree	Disagree	Strongly Disagree
I practise healthy habits in diet, exercise and sleep in order to be physically and mentally able to cope with the rigours of teaching.				
I am constantly learning, growing, gaining new perspectives and acquiring new skills so I don't become stale.				
I have rich satisfying relationships with friends and family and spend an adequate amount of time with them.				
I don't take on too much and I am aware of the dangers of burnout.				
I take time out in each day to have at least one refreshing break.				
I don't talk about my problems every time I go to work				
I don't live and breathe work. I take time to do things for myself.				
I spend time with people other than my colleagues.				
! seek help if I am finding it hard to cope with pressures from home or work, and take measures to minimise their influence on me at work.				
I take sick days if I need them!				

Be proactive	Strongly Agree	Agree	Disagree	Strongly Disagree
I have a clear sense of purpose and direction about what inspires and energises me.				
I plan, prioritise and organise so that I am not constantly rushing around in 'urgency mode'.				
I am a team player. I fulfil expectations of me as a staff member and follow accepted work protocols.				
If I encounter a problem with the functioning of the school or my performance, I try to do something about it.				
I seek help if I am having behaviour management or other problems at work.				
I am willing to have a go at new ideas and if I make mistakes I learn from them.				
I am willing to seek help from colleagues.				
I seek out professional development opportunities, and consider new perspectives to keep my interest in work vibrant.				
I am self-reflective and strive for improvement. I give myself 'think time'.				
I am doing everything I am capable of to optimise my job/life satisfaction and workplace effectiveness.				

Be realistic	Strongly Agree	Agree	Disagree	Strongly Disagree
I look at the big picture – 'There are many good things happening around here, most of my students do the right thing'.				
There are many good reasons for working for this school.				
I don't let little things annoy me.				
I don't take on too much and try to do everything.				
I am realistic. I am not going to get perfect student behaviour every day.				
I am realistic. Not everything is going to be just the way I like it.				

Classroom behaviour management checklist

The basics

Much has been written on behaviour management theory and we all have our own educational values and teaching styles. However, there are certain principles which we could call 'the basics'. I like the following ten principles as offered by McDaniel (1), as good basic guidelines for teachers to effectively manage student behaviour in the classroom.

1. **The focusing principle:**

   In effect, get everyone's attention before beginning the lesson. This may require a louder voice, a raised hand, or a bell; then the instruction can begin in a calm quiet voice.

2. **The principle of direct instruction:**

   This means getting the students on task quickly and keeping them on task consistently. One technique is to clearly state the assignment, the directions and the time constraints.

3. **The monitoring principle:**

   Keeping a constant check on student performance and behaviour. This means the teacher circulates among students and makes frequent personal contacts.

4. **The modelling principle:**

   Good teachers set an example for their students. Teachers who are courteous, well organised, enthusiastic and patient tend to encourage similar characteristics in students.

5. **The cuing principle:**

   Non-verbal reminders about behavioural expectations, such as a raised hand for silence, index finger to lips for a group of gigglers, or hands on hips for attention.

6. **The principle of environmental control:**

   A teacher can enrich, restrict, enlarge or simplify the classroom environment, according to the student's needs. A bored class may need enrichment; over stimulated students may need a simplified environment.

7. **The principle of low profile intervention:**

   Student behaviour should be managed as discreetly and as unobtrusively as possible, avoiding direct confrontation and public encounters with disruptive students.

8. **The principle of assertive discipline:**

   This means higher profile but non-hostile intervention. Assertive discipline is a combination of praise and limit setting.

9. **The I-message principle:**

   This results in clear communication between teacher and students, either by making specific requests as in 'I want you to ...' or by communicating feelings as in 'I feel frustrated.'

10. **The principle of positive reinforcement:**

    This means 'catch 'em being good'; ignoring minor misbehaviour while praising good behaviour.

(1) *Thomas R McDaniel*, A primer on classroom discipline: Principles old and new. *Converse College, Spartanburg, South Carolina, USA. Phi Delta Kappan, Vol 68, No. 1, September 1986.*

Why are my students misbehaving and what can I do about it?

The issue of human behaviour is extremely complex. However, in the context of behaviour management in schools there are some basic principles worth noting. Being aware of these principles can help us to understand why students behave the way they do, and enable us to develop effective behaviour management systems.

You have probably heard the catchphrase regarding the need for teachers to understand 'how students learn' in order to deliver effective learning programs. Perhaps there should be a phrase encouraging teachers to know 'why students behave the way they do' in order to implement effective behaviour management programs.

Below is an outline of reasons as to why students may be misbehaving. I have broken them up into three categories:

1. The student's basic needs are not being met.
2. The student is trying to achieve certain goals through misbehaviour.
3. External factors.

The basic needs of humans

Students may be misbehaving because their basic needs are not being met. There are many viewpoints on the basic needs of humans. Three examples are listed below.

Glasser describes them as:

- Basic physiological needs – food, shelter, safety
- Belonging and love
- Power – control/influence over your life and recognition
- Freedom
- Fun

Covey, Merrill and Merrill list them as:

- To live (physical needs) – food, clothing, shelter, health, basic economic means (money)

- To learn (mental needs) – learning, growing, stimulation
- To love (social needs) – to belong, to love, to be loved
- To leave a legacy (spiritual needs) – to have a sense of purpose and direction, to make a contribution, to know what values are important to you

Reilly also has a list which is similar to the above but which adds:

- Ego food – from success and achievement

And Carnegie adds:

- Sex (dependent on age and individual)

I have developed a list which is a composite of them all.

BASIC NEEDS LIST

Physical

- Food
- Clothing
- Shelter
- Safety
- Health
- Sex (dependent on age and individual)
- Basic economic means (money)

Mental

- Learning and growing
- Stimulation
- Power (control/influence over your life)
- Recognition
- Fun
- Ego food (from success and achievement)

Social

- To belong
- To love
- To be loved

Spiritual

- To have positive interaction with others
- Sense of purpose
- Sense of direction
- Making a contribution
- Sense of identity – knowing 'who you are' and what values are important to you

Can you identify any of your misbehaving students who may be lacking in basic needs?

GOALS OF MISBEHAVIOUR

Students don't always have a goal for their misbehaviour, but if their inappropriate behaviour is consistent they are probably trying to achieve one of the goals listed below. This is not a definitive list but can act as a guide for us to try and understand 'why students behave the way they do'.

Bennett and Smilanich list four goals of misbehaviour as identified by Rudolf Dreikers:

- **Attention** – student wants to be noticed.
- **Power** – the student wants to be in charge – typified by defiance, questioning, power struggles within peer group or with the teacher.
- **Revenge** – the student is revengeful and self-righteous. They want to be right and hurt others because they are hurting.
- **Assumed disability** – the student feels helpless and inadequate. They want to feel safe and misbehave to avoid failure – belief that they have no ability so they don't want to work (and fail).

Can you identify any of your misbehaving students who may be trying to achieve any of these goals–and are you playing into their hands?

EXTERNAL FACTORS

There may be other reasons why a student is misbehaving, such as:

- Under the influence of alcohol or other drugs.
- Medical conditions.
- Adverse effects of certain foods in their diet.
- Lack of social skills – have not been taught how to behave appropriately.
- Lack of self-discipline
- A group dynamics problem – see 'The problem class' checklist.

Or some people might say:

- A full moon.
- A windy day.
- A drop in barometric pressure.
- Alignment of the planets.

Who knows, there might be something in it!

ADDRESSING THESE POSSIBLE REASONS FOR MISBEHAVIOUR

1. We need to help students meet their basic needs through the provision of:
   - a positive school environment which is safe, caring and inclusive,
   - pastoral care and student services programs to help students in need,
   - appropriate and engaging teaching and learning programs which cater for individual difference, and allow students to be challenged and experience some success.

2. Make sure we are not giving students what they want (i.e. achieving their goals of misbehaviour) when we discipline them; e.g. attention, power, getting out of doing work.

3. Be aware of and minimise the influence of external factors which may be contributing to poor behaviour.

CONDITIONING STUDENTS TO BEHAVE WELL

People's behaviour is a reflection of their desire or urge to meet their basic needs and, as Napoleon said; 'is driven by self interest or fear'. Individuals behave the way they do because they believe that this behaviour will:

- ➤ lead them towards 'pleasure' (meeting their basic needs or reaching their goals of misbehaviour), and/or
- ➤ lead them away from 'pain' (discomfort or something they don't want to do).

Their strongest emotion at any given time will determine which way their behaviour goes – good or bad.

So, to encourage good behaviour ...

We need to condition students who misbehave into believing that:

- ➤ changing their behaviour will lead to pleasure,
- ➤ not changing will be more painful than changing.

Consequences for misbehaviour need to: lead to pain (discomfort, loss of privileges, or something they don't want to do)

- ➤ so that they associate bad behaviour with pain.

Good behaviour needs to lead to pleasure

- ➤ so that they associate good behaviour with pleasure.

For students who continue to misbehave, we need to ensure that they:

- ➤ realise that what they are doing is actually wrong or inappropriate,
- ➤ make the connection between what they do (good or bad behaviour) and their particular emotions at the time,
- ➤ have support systems available in order to develop strategies to help them break their pattern of bad behaviour,
- ➤ constantly reinforce their good behaviour with positives so they associate good behaviour with pleasure.

DIMENSION 7

RESCUE AND SUPPORT

Why are my students misbehaving?

Checklist

Refer to previous three pages for an explanation of this checklist. For students who misbehave, ask yourself these questions.

Basic needs	Strongly Agree	Agree	Disagree	Strongly Disagree
Are any of their basic needs lacking?				
Physical				
Food				
Clothing				
Shelter				
Safety (personal safety at home or at school)				
Health (health problems or medical conditions)				
Basic economic means (money)				
Mental				
Learning				
Growing				
Stimulation				
Power (control/influence over their lives)				
Recognition				
Fun				
Ego food (from success and achievement)				
Social				
To have positive interaction with others				
To belong				
To love				
To be loved				
Spiritual				
Sense of identity – knowing 'who you are' and what values are important to you				
Sense of purpose				
Sense of direction				
Making a contribution				
If any of these needs are lacking, can you help the student to meet them?				

Goals of misbehaviour	Strongly Agree	Agree	Disagree	Strongly Disagree
Is there a goal of their misbehaviour? If so what is it?				
To get attention				
To usurp power (control) from the teacher or the peer group				
To get revenge (to hurt others because they are hurting)				
Assumed disability – they believe they have no ability so they don't want to do any work (and fail again)				
Is your reaction to their behaviour helping them to achieve their goals? **Example 1, assumed disability:** If you send a kid outside, are they happy because they don't have to do any work? **Example 2, power:** If you send a kid straight to the deputy are you saying, 'I can't control you myself'?				

RESCUE AND SUPPORT

BEHAVIOUR MANAGEMENT

DIMENSION 7

External factors	Strongly Agree	Agree	Disagree	Strongly Disagree
Could there be external factors or other reasons for misbehaviour?				
Under the influence of alcohol or other drugs.				
Medical conditions.				
Adverse effects of certain foods in their diet.				
Lack of social skills – have not been taught how to behave appropriately.				
Lack of self-discipline.				
A group dynamics problem – see the 'Problem class' checklist.				

Conditioning students to behave well	Strongly Agree	Agree	Disagree	Strongly Disagree
Are you conditioning students towards good behaviour?				
Do you reward good behaviour with 'pleasure?'				
Do consequences for misbehaviour lead to 'pain' – discomfort, loss of privileges, or something the student doesn't want to do?				
Do they realise that what they are doing is actually wrong or inappropriate?				
Have they made the connection between what they do and their particular emotions at the time?				

The problem class checklist

Sometimes a combination of factors will make a particular class difficult to teach. These problems need to be identified and strategies put in place to address them. Below is a checklist of possible problems and solutions.

See also Dimension 3 – Relationships; 'Teacher–student, student–student relationship checklist.'

POSSIBLE CONTRIBUTING FACTORS TO A CLASSROOM DYNAMICS PROBLEM

The classroom

- Dirty
- Graffiti
- Untidy
- Old furniture
- Damaged desks
- Pin-up boards damaged
- Posters hanging off wall
- Unstimulating environment
- An over stimulating environment
- Temperature (too hot or cold)
- Distractions from other classes (e.g. PE or loud music, noise)

Students

- Low ability group
- Big class size
- Large numbers of known behaviour problems
- Strong peer group (i.e. they do a lot of different classes together, or have been to school together for a long time; e.g. country schools)
- Number of known 'non-triers'
- Personality clash with teacher

Teachers

- New graduates
- New to school
- Teaching out of subject area
- Relief teacher

Timetabling

- Time of day (e.g. after lunch)
- Long periods (too long for some)

Subject

- Practical subject (lots of action)
- Perceived by some to be 'boring'
- Students have to do the subject but don't really want to (e.g. some electives)

POSSIBLE SOLUTIONS TO A CLASSROOM DYNAMICS PROBLEM

- Organise for classroom (including desks) to be cleaned and graffiti removed
- Get to class early, tidy room
- Organise for desks and other furniture to be fixed or replaced
- Repair or replace pin-up boards
- Put up new posters (neatly and securely) and make room more pleasant
- Organise fans or heaters
- Approach other teachers in surrounding classes to keep noise down if possible
- Change classrooms
- Assign each classroom a teacher to look after it
- Put desks in single rows
- Create a seating plan
- Split up known behaviour problems
- Keep lessons very structured
- Keep lessons stimulating
- Make sure lesson content is not 'too hard 'or 'too easy'
- Negotiate lesson content with students

- Be extra well prepared (e.g. board notes beforehand)
- Get to class before students (if possible)
- Send behaviour problems to support teacher
- Anticipate challenging situations and have strategies ready to implement
- Pre-write credit or demerit slips, ready to issue
- Give lots of positive reinforcement for students doing the right thing; offer incentives
- Reduce your class size by setting an ongoing task for the whole class, and 'farming out' a number of students to support teachers. These students could be rotated so it is not seen as a punishment (e.g. 2 students library, 2 students computer room)
- Organise for a member of the admin. team to wander through your class a few times during the lesson
- If it's a long period, investigate making it shorter by swapping classes with someone teaching at the same time.

BEHAVIOUR MANAGEMENT

DIMENSION 8

REVIEW

Review, reflection and planning for improvement

In this section:

Data collection ◄

Review and reflection ◄

Planning for improvement ◄

Reviewing your behaviour management system

The type of review processes you can use to monitor the effectiveness of your behaviour management system depends on the mechanisms you have to collect data. The following documents use data collected from BMIS resources as outlined in Dimension 6. These include demerit slips, harassment notices and credit slips. Home room teachers tally the information throughout the term and summarise their results on the data collection sheets as outlined in this section. This data is then collated to produce a behaviour management report for the whole school.

How you collect and monitor data will depend on the preferences and circumstances of your school. These documents will give you some ideas as to how you might collect data and use those statistics to plan for improvement.

What purpose do the behaviour management report statistics serve?

The purpose of the behaviour management report is to monitor the effectiveness of the school's behaviour management plan. It aims to provide a 'snapshot' of student behaviour across the school, by identifying:

- the extent of positive reinforcement being given to students (credit slips).
- the extent of positive behaviour as indicated by the number of students not getting demerits or consequences.
- the amount of negative behaviour being displayed by students (demerits and harassment notices).
- types of negative behaviour occurring.
- Year groups which are causing concern.
- students who are causing concern.
- the number of students reaching consequences,
- trends in behaviour.

What then?

The BMIS committee meets once per term to analyse the statistics and can:

- Implement strategies to address identified areas of need.
- Modify the behaviour management plan to improve its effectiveness.
- Identify students at risk and ensure strategies from the plan are being implemented to assist them (students at educational risk safety net – see Dimension 7).
- Recommend a 'focus for the term'.

What can individual teachers do?

- If staff are unsure of any elements of the school's behaviour management plan, or unhappy with any aspects of its operation, they can approach a BMIS committee member with their concerns.
- Set their own personal goals; e.g., give out more credits for 'caring attitude'.
- Set class goals; e.g. 'to get 200 credits next term'.
- Recognise any 'at risk' students they teach and ensure appropriate intervention strategies have been implemented to assist them.

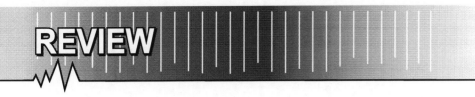

Behaviour management report – example

Behaviour Management Report

Compiled in an Excel® document

Term 3 2005

Summary

FIGURES AT A GLANCE

T1/98	T2/98	T3/98	T4/98	T1/99	T2/99	T3/99	T4/99	T1/00	T2/00	T3/00	
				2055	2095	2605	1373	3158	2747	2865	Credit boxes ticked
				6.34	6.4	7.22	3.1	10.1	8.12	8.95	Average number of credits per student
				531	1167	981	611	763	1215	916	Demerit boxes ticked
				1.68	3.61	2.98	1.92	2.43	3.59	2.81	Average number of demerits per student
				40	147	129	66	77	93	105	Community services given
101	135	130	127	37	112	89	66	64	97	69	Lunch detentions given
				9	10	13	23	11	12	9	Days of in-school suspension given
				5	12	10	5	0	21	0	After school detentions given
				17	9	41	42	11	12	16	Days of out-of-school suspension given
				10	11	15	8	17	6	7	Reported incidents of harassment
				10	36	39	19	20	30	22	Students causing concern (3 or more cons)
				160	144	98	113	151	89	110	Students with no demerits
				50%	44%	29%	35%	48%	26%	33%	Percentage of students with no demerits
				245	234	229	250	249	251	253	Students with no consequences
				77%	72%	69%	78%	79%	74%	75%	Percentage of students with no consequences
				316	323	329	317	314	320	338	Number of students surveyed

CREDIT SUMMARY

Highest 3 categories	Excellent class effort	567
	Responsible behaviour	374
	High standards in class work	305

DEMERIT SUMMARY

Highest 3 categories	Homework/assigns not completed	222
	Failing to follow teacher instructions	128
	No diary/not signed	105

HARASSMENT SUMMARY

Highest 3 categories	Teasing name calling	5
	Threatening with object	1
	Property taken or damaged	1

Celebrate Success!

Average number of credits per student	Up
Average number of demerits per student	Down
Number of lunch detentions given	Down
Days of in-school suspension given	Down
Students causing concern (3 or more consequences)	Down
Percentage of students with no demerits	Up
Percentage of students with no consequences	Up

CONCERNS

Number of community services given	Up
Days of out-of-school suspension given	Up
Number of harassment notices given	Up

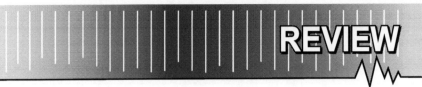

Tracking trends in behaviour – example

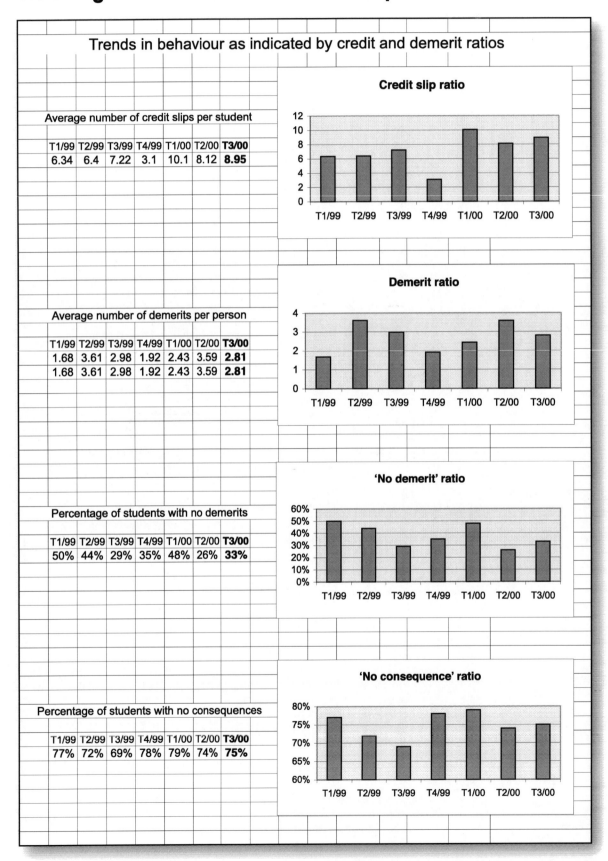

Trends in behaviour as indicated by credit and demerit ratios

Average number of credit slips per student

T1/99	T2/99	T3/99	T4/99	T1/00	T2/00	T3/00
6.34	6.4	7.22	3.1	10.1	8.12	**8.95**

Average number of demerits per person

T1/99	T2/99	T3/99	T4/99	T1/00	T2/00	T3/00
1.68	3.61	2.98	1.92	2.43	3.59	**2.81**
1.68	3.61	2.98	1.92	2.43	3.59	**2.81**

Percentage of students with no demerits

T1/99	T2/99	T3/99	T4/99	T1/00	T2/00	T3/00
50%	44%	29%	35%	48%	26%	**33%**

Percentage of students with no consequences

T1/99	T2/99	T3/99	T4/99	T1/00	T2/00	T3/00
77%	72%	69%	78%	79%	74%	**75%**

Using statistics in Excel® documents

Statistics in Excel® documents can help us see patterns of behaviour, which enable us to identify areas of concern and cohorts causing problems. The next step is to plan strategies to address these issues.

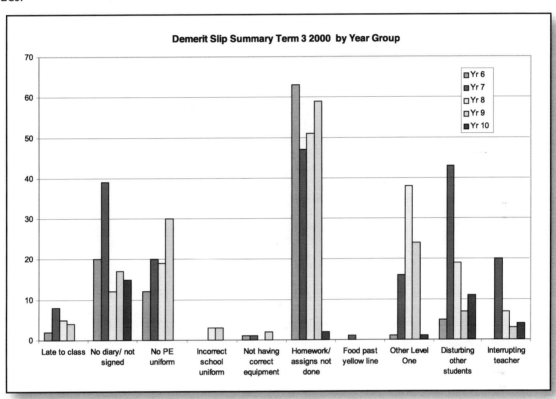

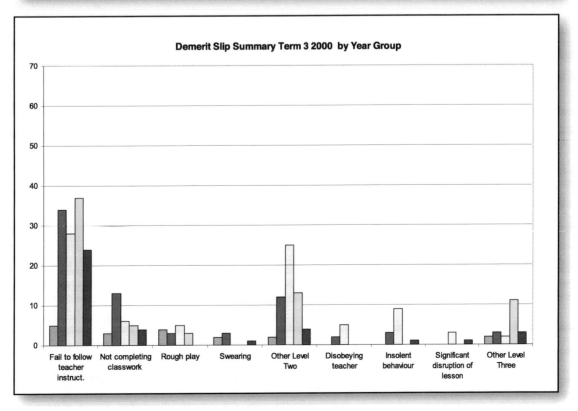

Responding to the data – Planning for improvement

The following notes come from a BMIS committee meeting which had reviewed the behaviour management report as per the example on the previous pages. It provides an example of how to plan for improvement after analysing behaviour management statistics. It should be noted that anecdotal data from committee members and other staff are also used to review the school's behaviour management system.

Behaviour management report – Term 3 Review and recommendations			
Issues identified	**Action to address issues**	**By whom**	**By when**
Homework	Should homework issues be made separate from behaviour management system; i.e. should teachers deal with it themselves? 1. To be put on agenda for the next staff meeting for discussion. 2. Homework committee to be formed to develop whole-school homework policy.	Bev Bev	Next staff meeting
Failing to follow teacher's instructions	1. To be put on agenda next staff meeting – Staff should make sure they are following correct BMIS procedures when dealing with students who fail to follow instructions. Staff should be encouraged to ring parents. 2. 'Admin. Alert' cards to made for emergency situations. 3. Apology note to be made up as a possible consequence of poor behaviour (Student apology note). 4. Need for cordless phones and no STD bar for emergency situations.	Bruce Dave Dave Fred	Next staff meeting By week 3 By week 3 By week 4
Student's attitude towards others	1. Code of behaviour to be modified to include care and courtesy; i.e. 'Care, courtesy, respect and responsibility'. 2. New clearer posters – more visual impact – teachers to reinforce. 3. Virtue of the week to be put in newsletter. 4. A caring schools Program to teach social skills to be investigated – meeting for interested staff.	Heather Wendy Sue Dawn	By week 4 By week 4 By week 2 Wed lunch week 3
Problems for relief teachers	1. Photo ID sheet to identify names 2. Questionnaire for relief teachers – what help do they need, what systems have been successful in other schools? 3. Develop a relief teacher report sheet for a summary of the relief teacher's day; e.g. work completed, good kids, bad kids, suggestions for improvement. 4. Make a list of all things teachers should leave for relief teachers; e.g. well planned lessons, keep lessons and organisation simple, class lists, where to find resources, classroom rules, a list of reliable trustworthy students, possible troublesome students, where to send them, seating plans, extra work for kids who finish early. 5. Develop a relief teacher support package.	Peter Fred Fred Dave Heather, Unnur	 Week 5
Giving out of credit slips	1. Issues to be brought up at next whole-school staff meeting: • Don't forget the good students. • Try to boost students with low numbers. • Don't forget to do lucky draws. • Should we reintroduce prize draws over the PA?	Dave	Next staff meting
Harassment	1. Teachers need to be reminded to fill out harassment notices	Bruce	Next staff meeting

Focus for the term

Plug the modified code of conduct:

Care, Courtesy, Respect, Responsibility

Focus for the term

Respect the property of others

Social skill/Virtue for the week

Honesty

Behaviour management toolkit   www.ricgroup.com.au   R.I.C. Publications

Home room records sheet – 1 (page 184)

- The home room records sheet comes as a folded A3 card and is kept in the care group (home room) file.
- This side (sheet 1) has attendance, uniform and diary records.
- The other side (sheet 2) has a credit section, and a demerit, harassment and consequence records section.

Attendance, uniform and diary records

- Used by home room teachers each day to keep track of attendance, uniform and diary.
- Use the legend at the top of the page.

Home room records sheet – 2 (page 185)

- The home room records sheet comes as a folded A3 card and is kept in the care group (home room) file.
- This side (sheet 2) has a credit section, and a demerit, harassment and consequence records section.
- The other side (sheet 1) has attendance, uniform and diary records.

Demerit, consequence and harassment records

- Home room teachers use the legend above to keep track of student's progress.
- As students reach the various levels of consequences, intervention strategies should be implemented as per the behaviour management plan.

Credit records (page 185)

- Home room teachers use the legend above to record the number of credit slips students receive.
- If a student reaches 20 credit slips, he or she should be issued with a bronze award certificate of appreciation.
- If a student reaches 40 credit slips, he or she should be issued with a silver award certificate of appreciation.
- If a student accumulates 60 slips, he or she should be issued with a gold award medallion.
- Home room teachers can photocopy this credit records progress chart and put it up in their home room so that students can keep track of their progress and get recognition for their positive behaviour.

(Enlarge it to A3)

Data collection sheet – credit records (page 186)

Data collection sheets are filled out by home room teachers at the end of each term.

Tips for filling out sheets

- Do one student at a time.
- Staple all BMIS slips for that student together (i.e. credits, demerits, community service, lunch detention, harassment notices etc.).
- Do one data collection sheet at a time.
- Get someone to help you.
- One person reads out each category ticked on the credit slips, the other person tallies it on the data collection sheet.
- The tallying person uses a ruler to make it easier to follow each row.
- Put in the totals at the bottom of each tally sheet.
- File your students' slips in your care group (home room) records file. If that gets too full, use a filing cabinet or an archive box.
- Have them readily accessible in case of parent interviews or if the student services team or deputy needs some background on the student's behaviour.
- Place tally sheets in BMIS coordinator's pigeonhole when you have finished.

Data collection sheet – demerit records (page 187)

Data collection sheets are filled out by home room teachers at the end of each term.

Tips for filling out sheets

- Do one student at a time.
- Staple all BMIS slips for that student together (i.e. credits, demerits, community service, lunch detention, harassment notices etc.).
- Do one data collection sheet at a time.
- Get someone to help you.
- One person reads out each category ticked on the credit slips, the other person tallies it on the data collection sheet.
- The tallying person uses a ruler to make it easier to follow each row.
- Put in the totals at the bottom of each tally sheet.
- File your students' slips in your care group (home room) records file. If that gets too full, use a filing cabinet or an archive box.
- Have them readily accessible in case of parent interviews or if the student services team or deputy needs some background on the student's behaviour.
- Place tally sheets in BMIS coordinator's pigeonhole when you have finished.

Data collection sheet – consequences and harassment records (page 188)

Data collection sheets are filled out by home room teachers at the end of each term.

Tips for filling out sheets

- Consequence records come straight off your home room records sheet.

For harassment notices

- Do one student at a time.
- Staple all BMIS slips for that student together (i.e. credits, demerits, community service, lunch detention, harassment notices etc.).
- Do one data collection sheet at a time.
- Get someone to help you.
- One person reads out each category ticked on the harassment notice, the other person tallies it on the data collection sheet.
- The tallying person uses a ruler to make it easier to follow each row.
- Put in the totals at the bottom of each tally sheet.
- File your students' slips in your care group (home room) records file. If that gets too full, use a filing cabinet or an archive box.
- Have them readily accessible in case of parent interviews or if the student services team or deputy needs some background on the student's behaviour.
- Place tally sheets in BMIS coordinator's pigeonhole when you have finished.

HOME ROOM RECORDS SHEET – 1

Attendance, uniform and diary records

✓ = present, A = absent, S = suspended, N = note, L = late, U = out of uniform, ● = diary signed, ✗ = diary not signed.

WEEK	1					2					3					4					5					6				
DATE																														
NAME	M	T	W	T	F	M	T	W	T	F	M	T	W	T	F	M	T	W	T	F	M	T	W	T	F	M	T	W	T	F

WEEK	7					8					9					10					11					12				
DATE																														
NAME	M	T	W	T	F	M	T	W	T	F	M	T	W	T	F	M	T	W	T	F	M	T	W	T	F	M	T	W	T	F

HOME ROOM RECORDS SHEET – 2
Demerit, consequence and harassment records

Home room _____

Term _____

	X = 1 demerit, O = community service or lunch detention given, ● = completed																					X = incident or no. of days detention or suspension														
NAME	LEVEL 1 DEMERITS								LEVEL 2 DEMERITS												LEVEL 3 DEMERITS			AFTER SCHOOL DETENT.			IN-SCHOOL SUSP.			OUT-OF-SCHOOL SUSP.			HARASS-MENT		
	1	2	3	●	4	5	6	●	1	2	3	●	4	5	6	●	7	8	9	●	1	2	3	1	2	3	1	2	3	1	2	3	1	2	3

CREDIT RECORDS

	✓ = credit slip, O = certificate due, ● = certificate given																																																	
NAME	1	2	3	4	5	6	7	8	9	10	11	12	13	14	15	16	17	18	19	20	21	22	23	24	25	26	27	28	29	30	31	32	33	34	35	36	37	38	39	40	41	42	43	44	45	46	47	48	49	50

		CLASS:	TEACHER:	TERM:
TOTAL	NAME			

	RESPONSIBLE BEHAVIOUR
	CARING ATTITUDE
	IMPROVED ATTITUDE
	IMPROVED EFFORT
	CONSISTENT CLASS EFFORT
	EXCELLENT CLASS EFFORT
	POSITIVE CONTRIBUTION
	WILLINGNESS TO HELP
	HIGH STANDARDS IN CLASS WORK
	HIGH STANDARDS IN ASSIGNMENT
	HIGH STANDARDS IN TEST
	SIGNIFICANT IMPROVEMENT IN ASSIGNMENTS
	SIGNIFICANT IMPROVEMENT IN TESTS
	CORRECT SCHOOL UNIFORM
	CORRECT PHYSICAL EDUCATION UNIFORM
	RETURNS NOTE PROMPTLY
	OTHER

DATA COLLECTION SHEET – DEMERIT RECORDS

				NAME																																	

CLASS:

TEACHER:

TERM:

LEVEL ONE DEMERITS
- LATE TO CLASS
- NO DIARY/NOT SIGNED
- NO PHYSICAL EDUCATION UNIFORM
- INCORRECT SCHOOL UNIFORM
- NOT HAVING CORRECT EQUIPMENT
- HOMEWORK/ASSIGNMENTS NOT COMPLETED
- FOOD PAST YELLOW LINE
- OTHER

LEVEL TWO DEMERITS
- DISTURBING OTHER STUDENTS
- INTERRUPTING TEACHER
- FAILING TO FOLLOW TEACHER'S INSTRUCTIONS
- NOT COMPLETING CLASS WORK
- ROUGH PLAY
- SWEARING
- OTHER

LEVEL THREE DEMERITS
- DISOBEYING TEACHER
- INSOLENT BEHAVIOUR
- SIGNIFICANT DISRUPTION OF LESSON
- OTHER

TOTAL

DATA COLLECTION SHEET – CONSEQUENCE AND HARASSMENT RECORDS

CLASS:

TEACHER:

TERM:

NAME																																	TOTAL

CONSEQUENCES		
COMMUNITY SERVICE		
LUNCH DETENTION		
CLASS WITHDRAWAL		
IN-SCHOOL SUSPENSION		
AFTER SCHOOL DETENTION		
OUT- OF-SCHOOL SUSPENSION		

HARASSMENTS		
TEASING/NAME CALLING		
VERBAL THREATS		
THREATENING WITH OBJECT		
NASTY LOOKS, SIGNS, OR GESTURES		
PROPERTY TAKEN OR DAMAGED		
FOLLOWING		
PHYSICAL INJURY		
SPREADING RUMOURS		
SPITTING		
WRITING INSULTS, GRAFFITI, NOTES, ETC.		
OTHER		

BIBLIOGRAPHY

Bennett, B., Rolheiser, C., Stevahn, L. (1991) *Cooperative learning: Where the heart meets mind.* Toronto, ON: Educational Connections

Bennett, B. , Smilanich, P. (1993) *Classroom management: A thinking and caring approach.* Toronto, ON: Bookation Inc.

Canter, L. , Canter, M. (1992) *Assertive discipline: Positive behaviour management for today's classroom.*

Covey, S. ,Merrill, A. , Merrill, R. (1994) *First things first.* New York: Simon & Schuster Inc.

Curriculum Council. (1998) *Curriculum framework.* Western Australia: Curriculum Council

Dreikurs, R. , Bronia, G. , Pepper, F. (1971) *Maintaining sanity in the classroom: Illustrated teaching techniques.* New York: Harper and Row

Education Department of South Australia, (1989) *School discipline: The management of student behaviour.* 'Promoting Responsible Behaviour'. Adelaide SA

Education Department Western Australia (1999) *Making the difference: Behaviour management in schools.* Perth, WA.

Glasser, W. (1986) *Control theory in the classroom.* New York: Harper & Row

Lewis, R. , Lovegrove, M. (1983) *Pupils on punishment*, SET Research Information for Teachers, Latrobe University.

McDaniel, T, (1986) *A primer on classroom discipline: Principles old and new.* Converse College, Spartanburg, South Carolina, USA. Phi Delta Kappan, Vol 68, No. 1, September 1986.

McGrath, H. and Noble, T. (2001) *BOUNCE BACK! A classroom program for teaching students to be resilient.* Melbourne: Pearson (Longman) Australia

McGrath, H. (2001) *Developing social skills and resiliency*, Faculty of Education, Deakin University – paper presented at seminar, Perth Western Australia

Reilly, W. (1983) *How to get what you want out of life.* New Jersey: Prentice-Hall

Rogers, B. (1995) *Behaviour management: A whole school approach*, Gosford, Australia: Scholastic Australia.

Morrison, B. (2002) *Bullying and victimisation in schools: A restorative justice approach*, Australian Institute of Criminology. Canberra.

R.I.C. Publications   www.ricgroup.com.au   *Behaviour management toolkit*   189

To order more copies of the *Behaviour management toolkit – a manual of good ideas and strategies for behaviour management in schools*:

- Visit www.behaviourmanagement.net
- Email admin@behaviourmanagement.net

To find more behaviour management resources and to download templates:

- Visit www.behaviourmanagement.net

To contact David Koutsoukis regarding presentations:

- Visit www.funman.com.au
- Email dave@funman.com.au